Before it Rains Anymore

Alec Mercer

Copyright 2025 © Alec Mercer

All rights reserved.

Alec Mercer has asserted rights under the Copyright, Designs and Patents Act 1988 to be identified as the author of this book. No portion of this book may be reproduced in any form without the written permission of the author.

Acknowledgements

I am very grateful to friends who read early drafts of this collection of stories and offered helpful comments, which encouraged me to make numerous changes. Perhaps with the stories written down, they will be spared from hearing them too often. The names of people mentioned in the narrative have been changed, and I trust there is not too much discrepancy between their recollection of events and mine. Many friends, colleagues, and people I met along the way enriched the experience of travelling in different countries, through their companionship or willingness to share information and stories. I would like to thank the team at A1 Book Publishing UK for their assistance in making publication possible.

Preface

The COVID pandemic affected the lives of millions of people and restricted the global travel that had fostered its spread. For the author, restrictions on movement outside the home during the pandemic allowed time for reflection on earlier experiences when travelling or working abroad. The incidents described here occurred over a period of fifty years in different countries in Asia, Africa, the Middle East, the Americas, and Australasia. Recalling incidents in places more distant than the local park, and especially writing about them, proved quite therapeutic. The stories came to mind through association or affinity, and this is reflected in the order here, which owes little to chronology. Although autobiographical, this is not a life story. Many significant events and people are not mentioned, and attempting to recall conversations from long ago would result in fiction.

The selected incidents are described as succinctly and accurately as memory allows, supported by a few notes scribbled down occasionally over the years. Some historical context is included along with the reason for being in a particular country at a particular time. The stories and anecdotes from very different pre-pandemic times could entertain readers of all ages who enjoy travel, including younger ones in their 'odyssey years,' and those rightly concerned about the carbon footprint.

England, November 2025

Before it Rains Anymore

The Congo, 1994

A four-seater plane descended towards a dirt landing strip on the northern shore of Lake Kivu in the Congo. We'd flown west from Nairobi that morning, over Lake Victoria and the spectacular volcanic craters of the Virunga Mountains. As the plane gradually descended, specks on the ground became recognisable animals, not zebra or wildebeest but grazing goats and cows just wandering around. I asked the pilot what he could do if one got in the way. "Not much," he said, "we'd just tip over if we swerved." As we got lower, I saw a white cow plodding slowly towards our line of descent. The ground rushed up to meet us, and the plane bounced, sending small stones pinging against the metal underbelly. We lurched from side to side as the brakes took hold. The plane steadied to a more earthly speed, and my heartbeat slowed. I could see the long horns of the white cow as it moved steadily away from the strip unperturbed. The plane came to a halt. After minor adjustments to switches and controls, the pilot cut the engines. "Welcome to Goma," he said.

Working for a medical relief organisation, I'd been asked to spend three weeks in Goma providing technical support for health surveillance among tens of thousands of refugees who had recently arrived during the genocide in Rwanda. With the pilot and co-pilot of the UN plane, I set off to walk a hundred metres or so to a couple of porta-cabins of the kind used as offices on building sites. As we approached this 'airport terminal,' three men emerged from one of the cabins and came walking towards us carrying bags. They were heading for another small plane parked by the strip.

We stopped to exchange greetings with the pilot and his two passengers, who were Japanese volcanologists. Wishing them an enjoyable flight, we walked towards the cabins. I wondered whether it was a good time to arrive. The volcanologists were leaving, but at least they weren't in a hurry. We drove the short distance into town, passing hundreds of makeshift shelters, crude wigwams of sticks and plastic sheeting spread out across a vast open plain. Plumes of smoke rose vertically from wood fires, and a blue-grey smog lingered in the hot air.

In the evening, after dinner with the rest of our team, I left the house alone and walked towards the edge of town. I needed some time to reflect on the bad news I'd just heard about one of the nurses on our health programme in southern Sudan. A few days earlier, she'd stayed in the house where I lived in Nairobi, before catching her flight to Europe for medical treatment.

It was growing dark, and the sky was heavy with the heat of the day. The kerosene lamps of street vendors cast long shadows on the ground. There was just enough light to guide my feet through piles of vegetables, clothes and household items lying beside the dusty road. I walked slowly through flickering shadows, hearing the murmur of disembodied voices bartering and chattering in the gathering gloom. My eyes were drawn to a deep red streak far above the horizon. The first thought in my tired mind was afterglow, but it was too high up and long after sunset. As my eyes adjusted, a dark shape loomed up ahead – a massive volcano smouldering and brooding ominously over the town. From the same spot the next morning, I could see no red glow, just a plume of smoke rising vertically in the still air above Mount Nyiragongo.

In May 2021, the lava flow from an eruption of Mount Nyiragongo stopped a few hundred metres outside Goma, a sprawling town of more than 600,000 people. Hundreds of houses and community buildings in the surrounding villages were destroyed, and several people were killed. A lava flow in 2002 had destroyed about one-fifth of the town and made over 100,000 people homeless. More than 200 people died from trauma, burns and carbon dioxide asphyxiation.

Cameroon, 1986

Some years before the trip to Goma, I'd travelled by bus from Bamenda to Bafousam in Western Cameroon while on vacation. The road passes Lake Nyos, the only sizeable body of water in the area, lying in the crater of an 'extinct' volcano. When I arrived in the capital, Yaounde, a couple of weeks later, I found a recent English-language newspaper in which the main report described a disaster that occurred a few days after I had passed by the lake.

On 21 August 1986, more than 1,700 people were killed when a cloud of carbon dioxide gas escaped from the deep waters of Lake Nyos. Being heavier than air, the gas rolled over the ground in an invisible cloud several metres deep. Nearly all the people in the villages around the lake suffocated in their sleep through lack of oxygen, and most animals and birds within 25 kilometres died. Gas normally leaks slowly and continuously from springs beneath the crater, but that night a huge bubble was released from the bottom, possibly by an earth tremor or recent heavy rain.

Cameroon had not been on my travel radar when I looked for a cheap long-range flight to have a much-needed break from work in London. I was getting bogged down in some independent health research while doing freelance fieldwork on social surveys to pay the rent. Before the internet, flights were usually booked through a travel agent, and I was surprised to learn that a very reasonable flight to Cameroon had just come on the market. I'd not been to Africa south of the Sahara, but had travelled in North Africa, Asia and Australasia. After reading an entertaining book by a young anthropologist who had recently spent a year in Cameroon,[1] I decided to take a chance and flew to Douala, not knowing what to expect on just a three-week trip. The following morning, I caught a bus out of the hot, noisy city, only to spend another sweaty night in a guest house near the coast, swatting noisy mosquitoes. It was time to find some cooler air in the mountains above their comfort zone.

The sprawling town of Buea lies in the foothills of Mount Cameroon, an extinct volcano about 4,000 metres above sea level. The coastal side of the mountain experiences extremely high rainfall in one of the wettest places on earth. In the surrounding area, rich volcanic soil supports banana, rubber, palm oil, tea and cacao plantations, and the valleys have good pasture.

It was late afternoon when the bus came to a halt in a small settlement on the outskirts of Buea, and I got out with a few locals. No smartphones in those days, so I asked directions from one of the passengers who spoke English. I had to locate the old colonial hotel where I planned to stay, and night falls rapidly after sunset near the equator. It had rained recently, and the main street was muddy as I walked past wooden shacks and *dhakan* selling vegetables, soft drinks, plastic buckets, brushes and other household items. A few old brick buildings were a reminder of the colonial days of British administration.

Fortunately, it was easy to find the old wooden building that had once been the retreat of colonial Europeans seeking respite from the tropical heat. Marie, a young African woman in her early twenties, greeted me cheerfully in reception and assured me I would have the best room. I was, in fact, the only guest and met few other foreigners travelling in Cameroon at that time. Climbing a short, creaking staircase to the first floor, we entered a large room with bare wooden floorboards and a few items of furniture – a chair, a wardrobe and a double bed that sagged a bit when I sat down, but the sheets were clean. I checked that the door and window were secure and agreed on the reasonable price, too tired to bargain. I noticed that only two guests had signed the register in recent weeks.

On the ground floor, a large wood-panelled lounge and dining area could have been the set for an old Gothic movie in a remote mountain location. No animal trophies on the walls, but the essence of a bygone era lingered in the damp and musty atmosphere. Two young African men sat talking at a table in the dining area, but apart from Marie and her friend Nadine, I hadn't seen anyone else in the hotel. By then, it was dark, and I had no plans to go out again after a long bus journey. Nadine offered rice and chicken in spicy African sauce for dinner.

While waiting for the cook to prepare the food, I drank refreshingly cold beer poured from a big brown bottle and chatted with Marie and Nadine, who sat opposite on a faded beige settee. They were curious to know how I could afford to travel to Cameroon, as they couldn't get good jobs to save money despite being recent university graduates. The talk of money made me think of the wallet I'd left upstairs in my daypack, so I decided to go to my room to fetch it before the food arrived. Unlocking the door and stepping inside, I came face-to-face with a young African man. He backed away, startled, and in a few strides, he'd crossed the room to the window. "Hey!" I shouted, grabbing him by the arm as he began to climb through. I held on, but he became suspended, and I had to let go. He dropped a couple of metres to the ground and staggered off into the darkness.

I looked around for my bag. It was still by the bed. The wallet with passport, traveller's cheques, and a few ten-pound notes had gone. I was angry that I'd left valuables in the room even for half an hour, although I'd shut the window and locked the door. My mind scanned through serious consequences, although somehow the situation didn't seem desperate. It was a small settlement, and the thief probably lived nearby. I went down to the lounge and told Marie and Nadine, who seemed genuinely shocked. I insisted we go straight to the police, and they discussed things in their local language. As they talked, they appeared to know something significant, although their manner wasn't suspicious. When I asked what they were thinking, Marie said the manager had been sitting across the room with his friend a few minutes earlier but they'd both gone. The three of us set off for the 'police station,' one of the few small brick buildings on the main street. It took less than five minutes to walk there. I was relieved to find an officer on duty, sitting grandly behind a huge desk in army-style khaki uniform. He agreed to go straight to the hotel manager's house.

Mountain Sickness

The policeman knocked on the door of a small wooden building, but there was no sound from inside. "Open up," he shouted in English. "Police." After a few seconds, a young woman came to the door, and the officer asked where her husband was.

Marie translated – "He's gone to bed sick."

"It's not true," said Nadine, "he was in the hotel lounge half an hour ago."

The policeman shouted angrily at the woman, "You go and get him." A young man came to the door almost immediately, wearing just a pair of shorts and visibly shaking. He appeared to have signs of the flu, although he was clearly not faking sickness. He stood forlornly at the door, a pathetic figure, trembling under questioning. He looked very scared and had no conviction in the story he was telling. The officer took him by the arm roughly and led him outside, telling me in English, "This man is a thief – I'm arresting him." The three of us walked back to the hotel, more confident that we were making some progress. In my room, I found my wallet on the floor. The manager may have dropped it when I caught him by the arm, or else someone had returned it. Everything was there, passport, traveller's cheques and money. Nadine came up to tell me the food was ready, and the rich spicy chicken tasted good with another cold beer.

In the morning, after a quick breakfast of bananas, tea and bread, I paid my bill and went to the police station to tell them I had my wallet. I saw the hotel manager in the lock-up by the side of the building, a kind of cage out in the open. He looked pitiful, shivering on the bare ground in his shorts like a neglected creature in a run-down zoo – it was cold in the mountains at night. I asked the officer on duty what would happen to him. "He will be tried and punished," he pronounced severely. "He will stay in a cell like that for three years." I said, the main thing was that I had my passport and money, so I didn't want to bring charges. The arresting officer arrived, and the two conferred in their local language. The more senior officer then accused me of organising the theft to claim insurance. I couldn't tell if it was a joke - more likely, he was aiming to get money from me. I said I would have to contact the British Consul if the matter wasn't resolved there and then, although I knew from experience there was little chance of support from Foreign Office staff.

I thanked the arresting officer for his prompt action, and the two men discussed things again in their local language. It may have been the prospect of complicated procedures, or the realisation that their superiors would get to hear of their ridiculous accusation, but they agreed to let the man go. Marie and Nadine arrived at the office, and we walked with the police towards the disgraced manager's house – no one spoke to him. I said it was time for me to leave as I had to catch a bus. There was, in fact, no bus until much later, but I was keen to be on my way. I walked to the edge of town and flagged down a pick-up truck. The driver was happy to take me to the main road, where, after a relatively short wait, I caught a bus up to Bamenda.

Indonesia, 1969

I checked in at a small guest house frequented by young travellers in Dili, Portuguese Timor, later the capital of East Timor. I'd taken the short flight from Darwin in the Northern Territory, Australia, in November 1969, planning to go by bus to Kupang on the Indonesian side of the island at the start of a mostly overland journey back to England. Unfortunately, I learned that the only land route across the island had just been closed due to fighting in the central highlands. The disruptive monsoon was also imminent.

The mountainous interior of Timor Island had been the scene of guerrilla resistance to occupying Japanese forces in 1942. When Imperial Japan surrendered after the United States dropped atomic bombs on Hiroshima and Nagasaki in August 1945, the Portuguese resumed administrative control of the eastern side of the island. From 1962–73, the right to self-determination was recognised in UN resolutions, but political parties remained illegal until the revolution in Portugal in 1974. Fighting continued until the Revolutionary Front for an Independent East Timor (Fretilin) unilaterally declared independence in November. Fearing a communist state on the island, the Indonesian army invaded East Timor, and it became a province of Indonesia. Guerrilla fighters once again waged a long campaign against occupation. Eventually, the Indonesian president, under growing international pressure, agreed to a period of UN administration, which led to independence for East Timor in May 2002.

The Monsoon Arrives

Due to the fighting in the central highlands in November 1969, the weekly flight from Dili to Kupang in the west would be the only way to cross Timor Island. Unfortunately, the plane failed to arrive as scheduled because the monsoon started early. The flight was rescheduled for two days later, weather permitting. The few young foreigners booked on the flight moved to a guest house near the airfield to be ready if the plane arrived.

It was relentlessly hot and humid the next day. In the sticky afternoon, the blades of an old ceiling fan creaked around slowly, barely stirring the heavy tropical air. The 1968 Rolling Stones album Beggars Banquet played on someone's portable cassette machine:

"… waiting patiently, lying on the floor, trying to do this jigsaw puzzle before it rains anymore."

A sudden downpour drummed on the corrugated iron roof over the verandah, and water cascaded into the garden. Guests ran out to splash around, enjoying the cooler air. Early next morning, the distant drone of a small plane prompted a rush to the airstrip − before it rained anymore.

Timor Island has an equatorial climate with two seasons − a reasonably cool and dry period from June to November and a hot monsoon season from December to May. The West Pacific Monsoon moves north into mainland Asia in the Southern Hemisphere winter and south to Australia in its summer. For most of the wet season, average monthly rainfall in Timor is 120-150 cms (47-59 inches) with considerable geographical variation. The arrival of the monsoon often causes a sudden switch from very dry to very wet conditions. Flash floods caused loss of life and much destruction of houses in April 2021.

After a very short flight across Timor Island, the small plane landed on a dirt strip near Kupang. The wheels spat small stones against the underbelly, and passengers clapped and cheered as the plane came to a halt. From Kupang, I travelled by boat to the island of Bali. After a few relaxing days there, I took another boat to Banyuwangi in eastern Java. On the long train journey west across the island, the cheap third-class carriage was crowded with people, goats and chickens. The recent song Marrakesh Express by Crosby, Stills and Nash came to mind:

"…travelling the train through clear Moroccan skies, ducks and pigs and chickens call, animal carpet wall to wall."

In Jakarta, I booked a passage on a ship going to Tanjung Pinang, 900 kilometres away on the island of Pulau Bintang in Sumatra. From there, I could get a ferry to Singapore. When the ship sailed a few days later, I was surprised to find two young women I'd met before were on board. Sarah from Australia and Liz from New Zealand had been on a boat from Bali to Java with me a week or so earlier. As we chatted, it transpired that Liz had flown from New Zealand to Australia, where she'd saved money for her trip to Indonesia by working in Canberra. Unknown to me, she'd taken over the job on population statistics that I'd done earlier that year to fund a trip to New Zealand.

New Zealand, 1969

From the air, the green volcanic islands and blue waters of the Hauraki Gulf looked spectacular as the plane approached Auckland in New Zealand's North Island. It was June 1969, and I'd flown from Melbourne after a year working and travelling in Australia in my early twenties. My plan to do postgraduate research was now on hold until I had the topic clearly defined. In Auckland, I took the first job I could find and rented a one-room apartment. Work in the aluminium factory was noisy and tedious, so after a couple of weeks, I phoned a market research company to ask if they had anything I could do that might be more interesting. The fact that I'd studied social research methods on my undergraduate course in London helped to get an interview. I was asked to go to their office in town straight away, so I set off wearing jeans and a T-shirt, which turned out to be appropriate for the job.

Landing in the Pub

The client was seeking advice on how to upgrade a few pubs in Auckland to attract more customers. The research firm needed someone to carry out discreet observational surveys in competing establishments, report on the décor, facilities and service, and compile descriptive profiles of the lunchtime and evening clientele. In those days, there were fewer regulations on drinking and driving, and a fashionable 60s Mini was rented so I could drive myself around town. Uncharacteristically restrained drinking relatively small glasses of beer, I spent the next couple of weeks touring the pubs of Auckland, all expenses paid. The establishment that scored highest in my review had comfortable armchairs and a TV in the lounge bar, which was unusual in New Zealand at that time. I was able to report that clear pictures of the Apollo 11 module landing on the Moon were a great attraction in the bar.

Just after 9.30 am (Eastern Daylight Time) on 16 July 1969, the three-stage rocket Apollo 11 was launched from the Kennedy Space Centre near Cape Canaveral in Florida. About 12 minutes later, the three-man crew of Neil Armstrong, Buzz Aldrin, and Michael Collins was in orbit around the Earth. After one and a half circuits, the rocket was fired towards the Moon, and three days later, it went into lunar orbit. To land the Eagle module in the Sea of Tranquillity, Neil Armstrong had to pilot the craft manually to avoid an area littered with boulders. At 4.17 pm on 20 July, with only 30 seconds of fuel remaining, he radioed Earth. "....The Eagle has landed." At 10:56 pm (EDT), Armstrong became the first human to set foot on another world. With more than 500 million people on Earth watching on TV, he climbed down the ladder and radioed – "That's one small step for man, one giant leap for mankind."

I lingered for a while in the convivial atmosphere of the bar, enjoying a brief celebratory drink with the other customers before heading to a more down-to-earth establishment that was way behind the changing times.

Australia, 1969

After travelling around both the New Zealand islands from July to September 1969 in the relatively mild southern hemisphere winter, I flew back to Melbourne. The aim was to cross the Nullarbor Plain to Perth in Western Australia, where I would find work and save enough money to travel back to England. I reached Port Augusta, about 300 kilometres north of Adelaide, where one road heads west to Perth and another branches north to Darwin in the Northern Territory. Neither 'highway' was surfaced at that time, and a cloud of dust engulfed me as a huge double-trailer road train pulled up close by. The truck driver, Jim, said he'd be glad to have some company on a journey of 2,700 kilometres, which would take three days, not to Perth but to Darwin.

We headed north on the Stuart Highway towards Coober Pedy, famous for its opal mines, passing the Woomera Prohibited Area where the British tested nuclear bombs between 1956 and 1963. Back in London in the summer of 1970, I got talking to a well-educated young Australian woman in a crowded pub in Notting Hill Gate. I was surprised to hear she was not aware that nuclear tests had been carried out in the country while she was at school there. A few years earlier, I'd seen a documentary on British TV showing a test explosion in Australia. British soldiers gazed with unprotected eyes at an enormous mushroom cloud that rose up not far away, high above the desert.

Information about military activities was most likely restricted in the 1960s as Australia was at war in Vietnam. The 'domino theory' of communist expansion through South East Asia had more credibility than in Western countries because of geographical proximity and the invasion of neighbouring countries by the Japanese within living memory, in the 1940s. When French colonial forces were defeated and withdrew from Indochina in 1954, the communist Viet Minh took control of North Vietnam, while the Viet Cong continued a guerrilla campaign against the US-backed government in the South.

Vietnam, 1999

I first got to travel in Vietnam on vacation when I was living and working in Bangladesh, thirty years later. I flew to Bangkok and, after an overnight stay, took the train up to Nong Khai in northern Thailand. From there, it was a short bus ride to the Friendship Bridge over the Mekong River, where I got a visa for Laos. A noisy tuk-tuk on the other side took me into Vientiane, the capital, where I found a guest house for a couple of nights. I spent much of the following day on the riverbank watching the boats, relaxing in the tropical warmth, and enjoying a chilled Lao beer at an open-air café. In the evening, I bought a ticket for the one-hour flight to Hanoi and travelled the next day, Christmas Eve. I was not expecting this special time in the West to be much celebrated in a formerly Buddhist country, now a communist state that had fought a horrific war against the Americans only a generation earlier.

The Vietnam War from 1955-75 was fought between communist North Vietnam, supported by China and the Soviet Union, and South Vietnam, supported by the United States and its regional allies Australia and New Zealand. US military advisers were sent in 1959, but by 1964, there were more than 180,000 American troops in

Vietnam. The Australian Government sent advisers in 1962, but soon deployed more than 8,000 military personnel there. Opposition within Australia grew after conscription was introduced in 1964, but there were other political objections. Some regarded the war as a continuing liberation struggle by the Vietnamese against foreign imperial powers — the French, the Japanese, then the Americans. The US and Australian governments viewed the war as necessary to prevent the spread of communism.

By 1969, the Americans were aiming to withdraw their troops from Vietnam and hand over conduct of the war to the South Vietnamese, but North Vietnam declared a Provisional Revolutionary Government in the South. After negotiations with the North Vietnamese, the US eventually signed the Paris Peace Accords in January 1973 and withdrew its forces from Vietnam by the end of March. Saigon fell to North Vietnamese and Viet Cong forces in April 1975 and was renamed Ho Chi Minh City. Vietnam became a reunified independent country in 1976, with Hanoi as its capital.

When I arrived in Hanoi on Christmas Eve in 1999, I found a festive atmosphere in the streets of an attractive, vibrant city. The tree-lined avenues teemed with cyclists five or six abreast and young families three or four up on small Japanese motor bikes. I found a room in a budget hotel with a balcony overlooking a busy street full of small shops. I was glad I'd brought earplugs. After a meal in a lively and friendly restaurant nearby, I began to feel more in tune with the festive spirit. Back at the hotel, I was greeted warmly by the manageress, who told me Christmas was a special holiday in Hanoi, particularly for the young who hadn't experienced the horrors of the war. They usually visited friends in the evening to exchange Christmas greetings and share some snacks. She insisted I go along with them as they toured other budget hotels to wish friends a happy

Christmas. The goodwill and celebratory atmosphere was infectious, and I went with the flow, perched precariously on the passenger seat of a Suzuki, weaving in and out of traffic along the crowded streets.

Australia, 1969

Years earlier, as I travelled north through the arid interior of Northern Territory, Australia, reports came on the radio about demonstrations against the Vietnam War in the major coastal cities further south. On the long road trip up to Darwin in October 1969, the double-trailer road train came to an abrupt halt in a vast, remote semi-desert. The truck driver, Jim, had pulled off the road because of a mechanical problem. "She'll be right, mate," he assured me as he unhitched the cabin from the trailers and set off for the last town we'd come through over a hundred kilometres to the south. It was over 40 °C, but bearable sitting in the shade with some drinking water and sandwiches, minding two trailers stacked with thousands of cans of beer. The silence of the timeless shimmering desert was serene, only briefly disturbed by a sound like a sudden summer breeze stirring the leaves of tall trees. A flock of budgerigars swished through the hot, still air of a treeless desert.

The following day, with the truck repaired, we arrived in humid Darwin around midday. I soon found a room in a downtown hotel with the coolest beer I could wish for. The next morning, I found the number of a mining company in the phone book and talked myself into a job testing core samples for uranium on the strength of five years of chemistry at school. Only days after driving past a nuclear test area, I started work in the laboratory of a uranium mine at Rum Jungle, about a hundred kilometres south of

Darwin. Staff accommodation was a few kilometres from the mine, which meant catching the early morning work bus. One morning, it came to a screeching halt in a cloud of dust. We all got down to inspect an enormous python that lay stretched out dead across the dusty track, its four-metre-long body flattened in two places, most likely by the wheels of a station wagon.

One evening, after a day analysing samples of uranium oxide in the lab, two colleagues and I drove into the bush to look for bats. We stopped and walked through the bush towards a rock formation and the mouth of a cave. A dense black cloud flapped by close enough to feel the draught. Entering the cave, we could see more bats suspended from the roof of a high chamber. With the beam of our only torch pointing down to guide our steps, we saw something on the ground a couple of metres ahead. We stopped dead – the python reared its head and we fled like 'bats out of hell'.

Undeterred, the following week we drove into the bush again to look for wild boar. Each carrying a rifle, we trekked for an hour or so along dried-up creek beds where our prey might be found. The air was still baking hot as the evening sun descended below a cloudless sky. Loose sand underfoot made walking strenuous, and enthusiasm was waning as we rounded a bend where the sides of the dry creek bed were steep. Suddenly, surrounded by startled snorting pigs, I heard the shout, "Don't shoot! Don't shoot." No chance of that with pigs and hunters bumping and barging together in a confused melee. Five or six squealing pigs scampered off before a gun could be raised, let alone fired. With food and accommodation included for workers at the mine, there was no need to hunt, and I was able to save all my pay. Towards the end of November 1969, I returned to Darwin to prepare for the overland journey back to England, which would take about six months on a tight budget.

India, 1970

Middle Class Crime

Travelling on the cheap in much of Asia in 1970 was not without risk, discomfort, and harassment from other passengers. Accidents were common on busy roads due to speeding and drivers taking risks when overtaking. Long-distance bus drivers had a reputation for using drugs to stay awake. Trains were a much safer option in India, with second class preferable to third to get a designated seat. On a journey from Lucknow to Delhi in second class, I had a brief conversation with a young Indian man sitting opposite. I said I was on my way back to England, where I would find work in London, and he told me about his accounts job in Delhi with a big company. He was interested in photography and asked if I'd taken any pictures in other countries. It was long before digital cameras, and I would have prints made from the negatives when I got to London. He asked to see the camera, and I showed him the old Kodak I kept in my pack. Feeling tired after a long day, I fell asleep with the pack on the floor between my feet. As the train slowed down in the outskirts of Delhi, I woke up and began checking that I had everything ready to get off. My camera had gone, and so had the young man opposite. With crowds of people in the station, there was little chance of finding him, so I checked in at a hotel nearby. With the help of an auto-rickshaw driver in the morning, I found the offices of his well-known international company in the modern business sector of that vast, sprawling city,

When I described my travelling companion to the receptionist, she called him on the internal phone, saying someone was in the lobby to see him. When he came in, his face went white with shock. I told the receptionist we had to go to his house to complete some business, as I was leaving that day. He informed his boss, and we set off in silence in an auto-rickshaw. At his father's house, he handed over the camera in abject silence, and his father pleaded with me not to tell the police or his employer. I said I would consider it and left for a late breakfast at my hotel, feeling relieved at the outcome. Later, I remembered a story a teacher read to us in primary school, Emile and the Detectives, in which a boy had his money stolen when he fell asleep on a train. With the help of some street kids in the next town, he found the thief and got his money back. [2]

Ecuador, 1988

Street Kids

Some years later, I flew to Quito in Ecuador to start a trip around South America and found a budget guest house in a hillside barrio. Despite being tired after a long flight, I went for a walk before dinner, carrying my camera in a small day pack. After exploring narrow lanes for about half an hour, I began to feel the effects of the altitude and decided to head back. I was suddenly confronted by two young lads brandishing knives. One threatened me from the front, while the other slashed at the strap of my bag from behind. I veered sideways to avoid the knife swishing dangerously close to my right kidney. The choreography was watched by a small group of youths standing a few metres away, although focused on the knives and holding onto my bag, I hadn't noticed them. After dodging and weaving for what may have been only a few seconds but seemed much longer, I decided it wasn't worth the risk and let go of the bag. As the two ran off, I shouted after them and tried to give chase, hampered by tiredness and lack of oxygen. I was quickly overtaken by three young lads about the same age as my assailants, who disappeared round the next corner. Before I got there, the three pursuers came back carrying my bag. After handshakes all round and much grinning, I went back down the hill to relative safety and dinner.

Quito is about 2,850 metres (9,350 feet) above sea level, just above the height at which altitude sickness can occur. At 2,500 metres, symptoms are not usually severe, but shortness of breath is common during physical activity. The disadvantage of visiting football teams not used to playing at high altitude is controversial, particularly for national teams playing in Bolivia's capital, La Paz. The city lies in a huge natural bowl at about 3,650 metres (12,000 feet) above sea level, surrounded by the mountains of the southern Altiplano.

Bolivia, 1988

After travelling on buses through Ecuador and Peru in March 1988, I reached Puno on the shores of Lake Titicaca. Its beautiful, tranquil waters lie about 3,800 metres (12,500 feet) above sea level, and the clouds seem to drift overhead unnaturally low in the sky. I was by then quite well acclimatised, and the spectacular onward journey to La Paz in Bolivia was enjoyable and largely uneventful. We had one brief unscheduled stop when a ragged, demented man dashed into the road at the top of the pass over the mountains. Fortunately, the driver reacted quickly to his antics and the bus screeched to a halt, allowing the crazy wild-man to wander off ranting at something no one else could see.

After a couple of days spent walking around La Paz and enjoying cold beers in a few of its bars, I took a very cheap flight to Santa Cruz in the east of the country on my way to Brazil. I planned to spend only one night in the notorious 'drug capital' before catching a train to the Brazilian border the next day. On the flight, I got talking to three men who looked to be in their forties and spoke fluent English with a Spanish accent. They said they were on a birding trip and lent me their guidebooks to help identify some of the birds I'd seen. After going through formalities at the airport, they invited me to share a taxi and stay at their hotel, but I'd decided to go to a small guest house near the station where I could get a ticket. After checking in, I walked around a couple of blocks and found a small restaurant nearby. It was getting dark, and this wasn't a town to be out in at night. I'd read a cautionary tale in an English-language newspaper a few weeks before the trip. The Santa Cruz football team had been playing a rival team from a nearby town, a game the visitors won by a late, disputed goal. As the players were leaving the pitch, the opposition centre forward who scored the winning goal was shot dead along with the referee. I did a very careful security check of the door and window of my room before going to bed, tired enough to sleep well.

The Bolivian drug gang Cartel de Santa Cruz, with headquarters in the town, was reportedly responsible for many narco-terrorist incidents in the 1980s. It was linked to drug trafficking organisations in Colombia, Brazil and Mexico. When the suspected head of the Colombian Cali Cartel, which also operated in Bolivia, was arrested in 1992, the Bolivian family Lima Lobo rose to prominence using land routes, river boats and aircraft to transport cocaine into Brazil. Illicit cocaine production in Bolivia increased, and Santa Cruz became a focus of transnational organised crime and a hot spot for drug-related shootings. Eventually, the suspected leader of the Lima Lobo group was arrested in Santa Cruz in 2019 on charges of international drug trafficking. He began a 15-year prison sentence in April 2020 along with his brother.

After breakfast at the guest house in Santa Cruz, I set off on the ten-minute walk to the station to buy a ticket. Those with no advance booking through a travel agent could buy one there on the day of departure. It was straightforward getting a ticket for the train to Quijarro on the Brazilian border, which would leave in the early afternoon. I had time for a walk in a park near the guest house, where I sat on a bench enjoying the cool morning air, listening to noisy birds squabbling in the trees. A man who looked to be in his twenties came walking towards me and sat down, saying something in Spanish I didn't understand. Pointing towards the station, I said, "El tren a Brasil," the only conversation I could manage at that time of day. I didn't sense any threat, and he soon got up and walked away.

Nada Señor

After collecting my pack from the guest house and checking out, I walked to the station with plenty of time before departure. Finding my seat by the window, I settled down to read about Brazil and watch other passengers boarding. After maybe ten minutes, a gruff voice close to my ear growled, "Policia." I looked up to see two men in civilian clothes standing in the gangway. One held out a card which appeared to be official identification.

"Qué?" I said, trying to appear disinterested.

He indicated that I should go along the carriage with them. I seemed to have no choice. When I pointed to my bag, concerned about thieves, one of them indicated I should leave it. Reaching the space between carriages, I asked, "Cual es el problema señor?" – the question I'd been formulating since I heard the word "policia."

"Traffico en narcotic", he replied gruffly.

I was not surprised but a bit concerned, as they ushered me into the bathroom, which was just large enough for three people to stand without touching.

"Nada señor," I said, holding out my arms, anticipating a search.

I was beginning to feel a bit shaky but tried to appear calm. One of the cops asked to see under my shirt, where I had a money belt around my waist.

"Nada senior," I said, showing them my passport and traveller's cheques, trying not to draw attention to the US dollars.

The cop said something in Spanish that I didn't understand, but I caught the name 'Lopez' a few times. I wondered later if 'Lopez' was the man who had spoken to me in the park. When the cop asked in broken English, "Why you walk to the station?", it was clear I'd been watched.

I said there was plenty of time before my train, and I wanted a walk before a long journey. I repeated my mantra, "Nada señor," opening out my hands. I sensed by then they would be after some money, but I was more concerned that someone would plant cocaine in my bag.

"Give us money", one of the cops demanded in English, pointing to my belt.

In some way, this was a relief as their cards were on the table. They were not threatening me with a gun, so I switched from polite compliance to being assertive.

"I'm going to Brazil and need the money," I announced.

Sensing that the train should be leaving soon if it was on time, I pushed past them to the door, opened it and went out into the corridor. As I walked back to my compartment, I became aware of the train starting to move slowly along the platform. I reached my seat without being followed and checked my bag, which seemed to be untouched. Greatly relieved, I sat down and took some deep breaths as the train began to gather speed. No one in the carriage appeared to take any notice. I expect people in Santa Cruz knew to mind their own business. I didn't see the cops again and assumed they had left the train when it started to move. I began to feel more relaxed, enjoying the atmosphere of an old-fashioned railway carriage. In the adjacent dining car with wood panelling, brass wall lamps and fancy shades, I ate an excellent steak and chips with a cold beer. Back in my seat, I dozed on and off, watching the gradual transition in landscape from dry scrubland and plantations to the watery marshes of the humid Pantanal.

Brazil, 1988

After crossing the border into Brazil at Quijarro, it was just a short taxi ride to Corumba, where I caught a night bus to Campo Grande. There was a chance to catch up on sleep on an all-day bus journey to Porto Velho on the Rio

Madeira, a tributary of the Amazon. The 'frontier town' and its river port later gained a reputation for cocaine smuggling, but in the 1980s, the local economy was based more on transporting soybeans. It was also the place to start a three-day boat journey to Manaus, an international river port hundreds of kilometres from the sea. Passengers were mainly locals who crowded onto two lower decks, but the more open top deck was the best place to sling a hammock and view the rainforest, birdlife, and wooden huts of settlers and indigenous people living along the riverbank. Three humid days and nights drifted along easily, lazing with a cold beer after meals heavy with carbohydrates. There was a chance to stretch and watch goods being loaded and unloaded across a wooden gangway at a couple of small river ports. The highlight was sunset on the third day when the Madeira River merged with the mighty Amazon. After a day in the busy port of Manaus, I headed north on buses along the dirt road through Amazonia to Venezuela, seeing little sign of the massive deforestation that was to come.

Brazil had an estimated 343 million hectares of tropical primary forest in 2002, the largest area in the world, and Bolivia had 40 million. Both countries had lost about 9% of this forest by 2022.

Cameroon, 1986

Travelling north on a dirt road in the northern hemisphere two years earlier, the transition was the reverse, from rainforest to grasslands with herds of goats, then semi-desert. After a day-long bus journey on bumpy tracks, the bus arrived in the market town of Kousseri in the far north of Cameroon, just across the border from N'Djamena, the capital of Chad.

By 1986, civil war in Chad and fighting to expel Libyan interventionist forces had devastated an already impoverished country. Disruption of trade and severe drought caused serious food shortages on both sides of the River Chari, which forms the border with Cameroon. Landlocked Chad is heavily dependent on imported goods passing through the border, while Cameroon imports food staples such as sorghum, onions and groundnuts from Chad.

I walked around the border town of Kousseri in the evening, looking for somewhere to eat. In the market area, a woman sitting by a food stall outside her wooden hut pointed to her empty pots. "No food," she said, shrugging in resignation. I found an old bearded man in faded robes selling mostly cigarettes at his small wooden kiosk. He sold me his last packet of six glucose biscuits at the usual price, saying, "You will find no other food in town."

Food supplies were threatened again recently when the movement of goods and people between N'Djamena and Kousseri was disrupted in April 2021. The president of Chad, Idriss Déby, had died after being in power for thirty years, and the Chadian military sealed the border. Déby was reportedly killed while visiting the army, which was fighting rebels opposed to his regime. Military leaders installed his son, General Mahamat Idriss Déby, as the new 'interim' president, precipitating further action by rebel forces.

In famine-stricken Kousseri in August 1986, I had the last packet of biscuits in town and a bottle of water to keep me going until I got back to Maroua the following evening, assuming the bus arrived in the morning. In the dry heat of early evening, I walked back to the ramshackle wooden building that was my 'hotel.' I'd taken my valuables with me but was relieved to find the padlock on the door and my pack still inside. Lighting the small paraffin lamp, I dined on biscuits and read for a while, managing to turn off the lamp before I fell asleep. Waking early next morning, I packed my bag and went out to look around the stalls in the market and the surrounding streets. There was no one selling tea, bread or any other food, but the early morning bus arrived and I headed south again.

Pakistan, 1992, 1993

At a neighbourhood street stall down a narrow, dusty lane in Peshawar, Pakistan, hot naan bread baked in an outdoor clay oven sold out quickly like proverbial 'hot cakes'. I was living nearby with a small group of expatriates working for a Dutch NGO on the United Nations (UNHCR) refugee programme for three million Afghans who had fled from war in their country.

The pro-Soviet government that came to power in Afghanistan following a coup in 1978 had initiated a radical programme that was anathema to the conservative Muslim population outside Kabul. Opposition in the city was ruthlessly suppressed, but by the end of 1979, large parts of the country were in open rebellion. The communist government had little control outside the cities and requested assistance from the Soviet government. Soviet troops and tanks reached Kabul on 27th December and staged a coup in which the president was killed and replaced by another pro-communist, Babrak Karmal.

Soviet troops occupied the cities, while the mujahideen waged guerrilla warfare in the mountains, backed by the United States and other governments opposed to communism. By the mid-1980s, there were more than 100,000 Soviet troops in Afghanistan and planes attacked villages and irrigation systems. With mounting Soviet casualties and diplomatic pressures, Mikhail Gorbachev withdrew Soviet forces from Afghanistan in February 1989, but support for the Kabul government continued until January 1992. The mujahideen who fought the Soviet Army maintained their opposition to this foreign interference.

In February 1992, I started work on the health programme for refugee camps in Pakistan's North West Frontier Province, now Khyber Pakhtunkhwa. Possibly a million Afghans had been killed in the war, and millions more were refugees. Our team in Peshawar soon moved into a large flat-roofed residential house within a high-walled compound, typical of those in better-off neighbourhoods. A similar house and compound in Abbottabad, not far away, became the last refuge of Osama bin Laden some years later. Through the barred grill over the front room window, we could see the garden, a patch of parched grass beside the driveway where our Toyota pick-up was parked. A two-metre high brick wall surrounded the compound, and a metal-plated gate gave access to the lane, which was just wide enough for one vehicle. A few metres along on the other side was a similar gate to the compound of our nearest neighbours.

Noisy Neighbours

One evening, soon after moving in, a few of us were sitting in the front room after dinner. A deafening 'crack' was followed by several more in rapid succession – unmistakably gunfire close by. Everyone got down on the floor below window-level in case bullets came through. The shooting stopped after a few seconds, but we called the local police on the landline. A man answered in English and assured us the police would come straight away. Amazingly, within a few minutes, we heard the sound of car engines in the lane and a voice shouted, "Police." About half a dozen khaki-uniformed men stood around outside the gate, some carrying old-fashioned rifles. An inspector, a large, imposing man with a traditional black moustache, was clearly in charge. He examined the metal plating on our neighbour's gate and the holes with metal edges pointing outwards. He proclaimed solemnly that the shots came from inside and banged on the gate. After a few moments, it was opened by two heavily bearded and turbaned Afghans. Behind them, two Kalashnikov rifles leaned against two chairs where they'd been sitting to guard the gate. They claimed to have been startled by a noise in the lane and, thinking it was an attack, they'd opened fire through the gate. There was no sign of other people or animals in the lane, but the smell of hashish suggested minds may have been elsewhere. The inspector fired off a strong reprimand in Pashtun with much gesticulating at the Kalashnikovs. He assured us we would have no further trouble, and if there was any problem, we should call him straight away. After handshakes all round, except with the Afghans, we returned to our house.

Gun Culture

A short drive from the residential house in Peshawar, we had a similar rented property for an office, a single-story, flat-roofed house with half a dozen rooms. Late one afternoon, I was preparing for a health survey in the refugee camps the following day. Colleagues had already left, and my office was quiet apart from the rhythmic creaking of the ceiling fan. Loud gunfire shattered the peace. The firing nearby stopped, and I heard gunfire in the distance, all around town. Localised gunfire was common in Peshawar, usually wedding guests firing Kalashnikovs into the sky to celebrate, but this sounded like an uprising. I phoned the house to warn the others not to go into town. They'd heard gunfire but didn't know what was going on. I checked the building again and went out into the courtyard. One of our Pakistani drivers was sitting in a Toyota pick-up listening to the radio. Pakistan had beaten England in the final of the Cricket World Cup.

The World Cup Final between Pakistan and England was played at the Melbourne Cricket Ground in March 1992. Pakistan's captain Imran Khan scored 72 of his team's 249 runs to win their first-ever World Cup when England were all out for 227. This success in a cricket-obsessed country confirmed Khan's status as a national hero. He founded the Pakistan Tehreek-e-Insaf (PTI) party, which ran a populist campaign in the general election of 2018. As the largest party in the National Assembly, the PTI formed a government with support from independents, and Khan became prime minister. In March 2022, the opposition won a vote of no confidence, and he was removed from power. In 2023, he was jailed for three years and disqualified from politics for alleged 'corrupt practices' relating to the sale of gifts from other heads of state.

I had a small room at the back of our office building and shared a toilet with a colleague whose office was in the adjacent room. One morning, I'd been enjoying the privilege of sitting in there, a luxury in that part of the world where squatting was the norm. On rising from the seat, I had difficulty standing, and my legs were shaking, throwing me off balance. Past experience suggested it was the start of a bout of dysentery or giardiasis, which can suddenly make you weak and dizzy.

Giardiasis is a parasitic intestinal infection caused by the protozoan Giardia lamblia, with symptoms of diarrhoea, abdominal cramps, bloating, and fatigue. Dysentery, an intestinal infection caused by the protozoa Entamoeba histolytica or the bacillus Shigella dysenteriae, is characterised by spasmodic abdominal pain, fever and bloody diarrhoea. Both these infectious diseases are highly prevalent in the tropics and sub-tropics due to people drinking unfiltered, contaminated water from wells or sources on the ground.

Unsteady on my feet, I sat down for a moment and then stood up again, leaning against the wall. I managed to get through the door and stumble along the corridor that led past the other offices. There was no one about, which was odd because we'd had an office meeting not long before. I made my way out of the building into the courtyard. All my colleagues were standing outside. The earthquake was over - no damage to the house and no dysentery for me.

In May 1992, a strong earthquake (Mw 6.0) destroyed many houses in villages about 75 kilometres south-west of Peshawar and in the town of Kohat. Reports indicated that 36 people died and about 100 were injured.

A Policeman's Lot

The following year, someone broke into the office safe, and we had to call the police again. A large amount of cash recently withdrawn from the bank to buy a used car had been stolen. The office 'fixer,' a local Pathan, thought the Afghan night guards were the most likely culprits. One of them didn't turn up for work that evening, and the view among the local staff was that he'd gone back to Afghanistan – the border wasn't far away. It was quite possible that someone in the office was involved, and a few people had suspicions about one of the local staff members in particular. Whether the absent guard was directly involved or knew something that would make him vulnerable was difficult to tell. Calling the police might lead to disruptive complications, but it could deter others.

Our old friend the inspector arrived and sent his officers to interview the Afghan guards and local staff, assuring us he'd "get to the bottom of it." We drank tea and chatted about crime in Peshawar. After a while, he began talking resignedly about his work, basically saying, 'the policeman's lot is not a happy one.' "We have to go down to the bazaar, quell riots, capture robbers and fight bandits…," he said, "…we have to haul them back to the police station… and then we have to beat them!" Black humour, but most likely true. The other night guard, a young Afghan, was duly taken away for 'questioning'.

The police modus operandi appeared to be, arrest the nearest Afghan, hang him upside down and let the truth come out. Afghans are notoriously tough and unlikely to give anything away. Our Pakistani staff thought the arrested guard was innocent. He was unlikely to have been directly involved as he'd stayed while the other guard fled. The following day, two of us went to see the inspector, who assured us there would be no beating or hanging upside down, but locking someone up for a few days might encourage others to talk. I went to the police station again the next day and persuaded the inspector to release the man. I had to accompany him to the court to retrieve the case papers, which involved paying the clerk to hand them over. The senior official with the authority to sign the release order also had to be paid. The young guard was eventually released a day or so later. Sadly, some weeks after that, we read in the local newspaper that the inspector had been shot dead on the doorstep of his house, reportedly by two Afghans. A picture of his face and another of his bullet-riddled body appeared on the front page. We never found out why he was shot, but with the prevailing gun culture, it was no great surprise.

Power Struggles

The national 'sport' for Afghans is Buzkashi, an old Mongol game played with a decapitated goat or calf used as the 'ball.' Two teams of men on horseback compete fiercely for possession. One afternoon, a few of us joined the crowd of refugees and local Pashtuns at a ground on the outskirts of Peshawar. After much wild jostling and manoeuvring, one skilled horseman emerged from the melée of horses and riders and galloped away to the goal, holding the dead animal by one of its legs. It could be a metaphor for power struggles and leadership rivalry between ethnic, religious, regional, and political factions in Afghanistan. [3]

The mujahideen fighters who had rebelled against atheistic communism and foreign intervention aimed to form an Islamic government, but rival factions fought for control when they entered Kabul in April 1992. They were unable to form an interim government as proposed under the Peshawar Accord, and fierce fighting continued in Kabul.

Afghanistan, 1993, 1970

Amid continuing insecurity in Afghanistan in 1993, representatives of relief organisations in Pakistan were called to a meeting with Afghan warlords in Jalalabad. The objective was to establish camps for displaced people inside the country, as there were already three million Afghan refugees in Pakistan. We crossed into Afghanistan through the Khyber Pass in our station wagon and followed a pick-up truck full of mujahideen standing with rocket launchers pointing to the sky. The dusty road to Jalalabad was strewn with stones, potholes and a few burned-out Soviet tanks.

A new peace agreement made in Jalalabad in May 1993 failed to end the fighting. Fierce fighting between rival mujahideen factions resulted in thousands of civilian deaths, food shortages and a disaffected population. A new movement began to emerge in Kandahar, whose aim was to impose sharia law and set up a unifying Islamic government. With support from Pakistan, the Taliban (students of Islam) captured Kabul in September 1996. They began ruthlessly enforcing strict codes of behaviour on the civilian population, particularly on women. The Taliban allowed the al-Qaeda leader Osama bin Laden to return to Afghanistan in May 1996 from his base in Sudan. He declared war against the Americans, who had military bases in his country, Saudi Arabia, the home of Mecca and Medina, the holiest places in Islam.

By that time, there was only one mujahideen faction capable of offering resistance to the Taliban – the Northern Alliance led by Ahmed Shah Massoud, an ethnic Tajik. His fighters had held out against the Soviets in the Panjshir Valley. He had come to view the Taliban and al Qaeda as enemies who had given the West a bad impression of Islam. He visited Europe in April 2001 and addressed the European Parliament, warning of an imminent attack on the United States. Two days before the attack by al-Qaeda on 11 September, Massoud was assassinated in Panjshir by two suicide bombers posing as journalists.

Kabul Café

Years before the Soviet–Afghan War, I'd travelled through the Khyber Pass to Jalalabad in 1970, in the old bus that ran from Landi Kotal on the Pakistan side of the border with Afghanistan. Bearded Afghans in turbans rode 'shotgun' on the roof with rifles – no rocket launchers in those days. Travelling across the country, I'd stayed briefly in Jalalabad, Kabul, Kandahar and Herat on my overland journey back to England from Australia. In a back-street café in Kabul, I drank tea with a French travelling companion while turbaned locals bubbled tobacco smoke through hookah pipes. A strong draft of hot air wafted down from the rapidly rotating blades of a fan suspended from the low ceiling. The whole rickety assembly rocked noisily as the blades whirled round. Rising carelessly from a seat with no protective turban could prove fatal. Women did not wear turbans and were not allowed in the café.

A new constitution in 1964 had granted women equal rights, including voting and running for office, and the Kabul middle classes enjoyed a 'westernised' lifestyle for a few years. Women outside Kabul and other major cities were denied those freedoms, and most people were living in poverty. Women had long been marginalised with a subordinate status in Afghanistan. Cultural roots of oppression, conservative patriarchal and religious forces, political instability and wars had undermined attempts to implement reforms. Efforts to improve the circumstances of women suffered a more serious setback when the ultraconservative Taliban came to power in 1996. Women were forbidden to work or leave the house without a male escort and forced to cover themselves from head to foot in public.

Central America, 2011

Years later, I was reminded of the café in Kabul by the rotating ceiling fan in a café in Chiapas, south-west Mexico. The owner's T-shirt offered encouraging advice. 'Face your fears and follow your dream.' The threat of robbery was a concern in parts of Mexico, Guatemala and Honduras, but the allure was colourful old colonial towns - San Cristobal de las Casas, Lago de Atitlan, Antigua. Ordering breakfast after a long overnight bus ride, I asked for huelo frito instead of huevo frito, fried ice-cream, not fried egg, which caused much mirth. I was served real fried eggs and some excellent coffee. The ceiling fan gently stirred the warm air, unlike the whizzing blades in Kabul that might have driven a small aeroplane.

Madagascar, 2004

Big Man, Little Plane

A tiny one-seater plane about three metres long was an attraction in the gardens of a restaurant near Antananarivo, the capital of Madagascar. I asked a group of French people at the next table if it was the president's plane. I'd just seen the Big Man's Mercedes with a vast fleet of black limousines when he was opening a new road nearby in July 2004. A few years earlier, the presidential plane would have needed two seats as the country had two presidents.

Following the election in Madagascar in December 2001, officials declared that no candidate had won the required 50% of votes. After a recount, the challenger, a millionaire businessman, Marc Ravalomanana, was declared the winner with 51% of the vote. The incumbent president of twenty-five years, Didier Ratsiraka, received only 36% of the vote, but refused to accept the result and relocated his 'government' to the east of the island. The divisive political antics that followed had disastrous consequences for the national economy and reduced the living standards of the people of Madagascar, most of whom were already poor.

United States, 2020

Divisive political antics threatened democracy and social stability in the United States after the election in November 2020. The incumbent president, Donald Trump, also a millionaire businessman, refused to accept that he'd lost despite the official count showing that he had seven million fewer votes than his rival, Joseph Biden. He encouraged supporters to protest the result in Washington, and thousands gathered on Capitol Hill on 6 January 2021. Hundreds of his supporters were filmed breaking into the Capitol building, causing damage and threatening elected representatives who had to seek shelter in fear for their lives. The incursion resulted in the deaths of five people.

Trump had won the presidential election in 2016 with three million fewer votes than his opponent, Hilary Clinton, who accepted the result. The unique 'electoral college' system for presidential elections in the United States ensures that the majority view in each state is represented, but the result is not decided by the total number of individual votes cast for a candidate nationally. Some smaller states have a disproportionate influence on the result. Trump had considerable support in the so-called 'rust-belt' areas where heavy industries had declined. New jobs had not been created after the global financial crisis of 2007−2008, precipitated by high-risk mortgage lending in the United States.

England, 2007

By early 2007, a house price 'bubble' had already deflated in many parts of the United States, but in England, 'house buying mania' persisted and prices continued to rise. Plans to buy a house after working abroad for many years had to go on hold. The feverish rise in prices finally peaked in August 2007 at the height of the hot summer. By the end of that year, it was clear that economic chaos would continue due to the crisis in the international banking system.

In February 2008, the UK Government nationalised one of the major banks to prevent it from going bankrupt. The bank's cash reserves were not sufficient to meet the demand for withdrawals when customers became concerned that their savings were at risk. To prevent a collapse in the interconnected banking system, the Labour Government had little choice but to subsidise a bank that had expanded recklessly and gambled people's savings on risky investments. Ironically, the bank was called Northern Rock.

Patagonia, 2008

Suspending house hunting in the midst of the financial crisis, I flew to Santiago in Chile at the end of February 2008. Mature leadership and management of the national finances by the first female president of the country, Michelle Bachelet, had prevented economic disaster, and the capital seemed relatively calm in the warmth of the southern hemisphere summer. I travelled by bus to Puerto Montt, further down the Pacific coast. At the offices of a shipping line, I was able to negotiate a reasonable price for a berth on a cruise ship for one night, as a passenger would be boarding further south. Sailing along the Pacific coastline of Chile afforded spectacular views of conical snow-capped volcanoes and the mountains of the southern Andes.

Meal Ticket

Disembarking the next day, I hiked for a while and found a guest house where I could stay the night. The following morning, I travelled by bus into Argentina and caught another bus down to Patagonia, the rugged region that tapers down to the tip of South America. The aim was to hike in the mountains of Torres del Paine, back on the Chilean side of the peninsula. On the way, I visited the spectacular Perito Moreno Glacier and watched giant blocks of ice break off its vertical face and crash into the Canal de los Témpanos. A couple of days later, I arrived in Puerto Natales in Chile and the next morning took the early bus to the mountainous national park. After checking in at the only budget lodge, I had the rest of the day to hike and climb in spectacular mountains. Towering pinnacles of granite, like giant termite mounds, rose almost vertically to about 3,000 metres. By mid-afternoon, I'd climbed as high as I could without special equipment and rested a while amid the silent grandeur of jagged peaks above a glacier. Descending was much easier, and in the late afternoon, I reached the lodge tired but elated.

After a short rest, I went to the reception to get a pass for dinner at the restaurant in a separate building. When I asked how far it was, the receptionist just waved vaguely down the track, which suggested it wasn't far. After a while, it seemed a lot further than I'd expected, but the ground was flat and walking at a leisurely pace in the cooler evening air was pleasant. I carried on despite tired legs and eventually reached a large modern building and went in through tall glass doors. I showed my dinner pass at reception and found my way to the large dining room full of guests having dinner. It was clearly a smart hotel for upmarket tourists. When I gave the pass to the dining room manager, she looked bemused but showed me to a table. I ordered a very large beer and collected food from a mouth-watering display of dishes laid out on buffet tables.

The manager returned, still confused about the pass. I explained that I'd paid for a night at the lodge, which included dinner, but would pay for the litre of beer. After an excellent meal and a refreshingly cold beer, I walked back to the lodge and slept well after all the exercise. In the morning, I went to reception to collect a pass for breakfast and was told they'd been contacted by the hotel about the dinner I had the night before. I had, of course, gone to the wrong place. Fortunately, I wasn't asked to pay for the five-star meal and enjoyed telling the story over breakfast at the much more modest canteen just down the track from the lodge. After an adequate breakfast, I hiked back to the lake to catch the bus to Puerto Natales, feeling slightly disappointed that I hadn't seen a condor. As I sat waiting for the bus, one of these majestic black vultures soared overhead, and half a dozen more glided over a ridge and down across the valley.

Later that year, after touring around Spain in a campervan, I was on my way back to England at the end of the northern hemisphere summer. Driving towards the Pyrenees through Aragon, I pulled off the road onto the edge of a cliff to look out across a huge valley towards the mountains in the distance. As I came to a halt with a sheer drop of several hundred metres just ahead, four lammergeyer, handsome brown and orange vultures the size and shape of a golden eagle, launched off the cliff side by side and swooped down over the valley.

England, 2008

Between the trip to Patagonia and driving around Spain, I spent the spring and summer of 2008 in England, still looking to buy a property to have a base there. Although prices had been falling since August 2007, there was great economic uncertainty in the worst recession since World War Two. Companies, both large and small, were going bankrupt, and thousands of people lost their jobs.

The source of the recession was a relaxation in the regulation of banking in line with the prevailing 'free market' ideology. High-risk, reckless lending in the United States fuelled a boom in house prices when 'subprime' mortgages were sold to people with low credit ratings. Many were unable to pay the higher mortgage costs when interest rates increased again and lenders repossessed the properties. With cheap loans no longer available, the 'housing bubble' deflated, sales declined, and property prices fell.

There were further economic consequences as banks and other financial institutions had invested in bonds that incorporated subprime mortgage debt. These so-called mortgage-backed 'securities' were downgraded in 2007, with some becoming 'toxic' and effectively worthless. Many banks and institutional investors sustained huge financial losses. The trust between banks, on which the interconnected banking system depended, began to dissolve. The normal day-to-day cash flow between banks was disrupted, and financial institutions and businesses were unable to access the short-term credit they needed to operate.

The global 'credit crunch' left banks in England unable to support businesses when they needed temporary finance. In 2008, house builders with contractors to pay sold finished properties at discount prices to cash buyers. In August, I bought a new apartment with savings from working abroad for several years. This meant I was free to travel for pleasure in the campervan I'd virtually lived in while looking for a more permanent base in England.

Spain, 2008

In the late summer of 2008, I drove south from the French Pyrenees towards northern Catalunya. The temperature rose as the road wound down through the small principality of Andorra. The landscape was changing dramatically from the green tree-covered mountains behind to the vast arid plains ahead. I stopped outside a village to look out across a huge straw-coloured field of stubble. The heat was intense after the cool air up in the mountains earlier that morning. A few dusty bushes marked the edge of the field where wheat had recently been cropped, and the brown hills beyond were dotted with almond trees. A single swallow swerved and swooped over sun-faded stalks, catching insects on the wing. In the nearby village, the chatter of sparrows in the bushes and the cooing of a dove were the only sounds I could hear in the hot still air.

In the dry and dusty hills, much further south near Almeria in Andalucia, I looked down on the fake settlement where 'paella westerns' had been filmed. The set had wooden stores, a bank, a courthouse and a bar, but no cowboys, no women in fancy bonnets or buxom barmaids. The empty dusty street blended with the semi-desert setting. A few wigwams stood proud only metres from the fake wooden houses of the 'white-folk.' The false neighbourly proximity belied the tragic history of hunter-gatherer people displaced by European settlers in the Americas, Australia and Africa. Harassment and murder of indigenous people continues in much of Latin America as they try to defend their traditional lands from encroachment and the hired hands of powerful corporations.

When Jair Bolsonaro became president of Brazil in 2019, he referred to indigenous people as 'outcasts' to be treated like terrorists. His government sanctioned violence against them and the illegal occupation of their lands by agri-business and mining companies. Bolsonaro announced that their land would be opened up for large-scale agriculture, and the area of rainforest cleared in the first six months of his tenure was double that in the same period of 2017. When Lula da Silva was elected and installed as president for the third time in January 2023, he vowed to haul Amazonia out of centuries of violence, economic 'plundering' and environmental devastation. Six indigenous territories were demarcated, forest clearance fell sharply, and a paramilitary campaign was initiated against mining in the territory of the Yanomani people.

Costa Rica, Cuba and the United States, 2009

The arid terrain and intense heat in southern Spain seemed to warn of severe consequences for South America if deforestation continued there. After returning to England at the end of 2008, I flew to San Jose in Costa Rica in January. The country is of particular interest because of efforts to protect the natural environment, a commitment to health and social services, and a higher average life expectancy than in the United States. I spent a few days hiking in the volcanic region around La Fortuna, before taking a bus across the verdant mountains of the Cordillera de Tilaran. Exotic birdlife and mammals are a great attraction in the Monteverde cloud forest around Santa Elena and in the spectacular national parks along the coast to the south-east of Puntarenas. Crossing into Panama, I took a bus up to Boquete and spent a day hiking in the mountain rainforest before heading up to the island of Bocas del Toro and the national parks on the Caribbean coast of Costa Rica.

Returning to San Jose, I was able to book a relatively cheap flight to Havana, the capital of Cuba, another low/middle-income country with a higher average life expectancy than the United States, despite a trade embargo imposed by its powerful neighbour for ideological reasons. After years of restrictions on foreigners by the Cuban authorities, it was possible to travel freely and independently on public transport, staying in private accommodation, usually a room in a professional family's house. After two weeks visiting colourful old colonial towns – Cienfuegos, Trinidad, and

Bayamo, I flew to Miami to connect with my return flight to London.

The United States economy was in deep recession following the financial crisis of 2007–2008. The global bank Lehman Brothers went bankrupt in September 2008 in the absence of Government or Central Bank support. Gordon Brown's Labour Government in the UK was the first to intervene to avert an imminent collapse of the global banking system when he announced a rescue package of £500 billion (US$850 billion) in October 2008. This massive 'bank bailout' supported by the Bank of England prevented bankruptcies among major banks and businesses dependent on their services. The Republican Administration in the US, led by George W Bush, followed with a similar bank bailout, and provided huge financial support for large motor manufacturing and insurance companies. Barack Obama continued these measures when he became president in January 2009, and added an $800 billion economic stimulus package to revive an economy already in deep recession.

In Transit in Miami

When I arrived at Miami airport from Havana in mid-March 2009, the country was still on high security alert because of the attack by al-Qaeda on the World Trade Centre in New York in 2001, and the ongoing military operations in Iraq after the overthrow of Saddam Hussein in 2003. Instead of waiting in a transit lounge for an onward flight, which is the usual procedure, transit passengers had to pass through customs and immigration control and undergo the rigorous security checks for other departing passengers. I was not asked a routine question posed when I first visited in 1972 – "Are you or have you ever been a member of the communist party?" and after showing my passport and flight ticket, I was effectively in the United States. I could have walked out of the airport building, taken a taxi into town and become another illegal immigrant. Instead, I passed through security screening with other departing passengers and presented my passport to leave the country. As the officer flicked impatiently through the pages, he asked quite aggressively, "Why did you go to Cuba?" The American Government did not allow its citizens to go to Cuba, but I was a British citizen returning to England, not seeking to enter the United States.

"It's an interesting country and I had a very enjoyable visit," I replied.

"It's communist," he announced.

"It has a good health care system," I said. Fortunately, that was the end of the exchange, and I was waved dismissively through the checkpoint to continue my journey.

State intervention in the UK and the US in 2008–2009 arguably prevented a collapse in the international economic system comparable to that leading to the 'Great Depression' of the 1930s. Despite its effective response to the banking crisis, which saved the jobs and savings of many people in the UK, the Labour Government of Gordon Brown was voted out in the general election of 2010. The incoming Conservative Government, opposed to Government debt, made drastic cuts in public services and began passing on the banks' debts to taxpayers, reducing the economic standard of living of many people for years to come.

India, 1996

In Transit in Bangalore

Some years earlier, on a trip to southern India to review health projects with a colleague, we were in transit in the relatively prosperous city of Bangalore. There was time between flights to take a taxi into town and have some lunch. In a modern air-conditioned restaurant, we ordered curries and chatted over a beer about the projects which focused on preventive measures. Jean sat opposite on a plush double seat upholstered in brown leather. Next to me sat an enormous grey rat. I turned my head to confirm what I'd glimpsed out of the corner of my eye. The rat gazed back unperturbed, and I thumped the seat to scare it away. It bounced, landed and sat still. I caught the eye of the waiter as he came out of the kitchens. "There's a rat on my seat," I said, as casually as I could. He came over looking disinterested and flicked an immaculately white serving towel at the rat, which scurried across the floor to the kitchens, most likely its home.

In a farcical episode of the BBC TV comedy, 'Fawlty Towers' broadcast in October 1979, the manic proprietor of a small hotel on the south coast of England, Basil Fawlty, played by John Cleese, is in serious trouble after a routine visit by the health inspector. The future of his outwardly respectable establishment is in doubt when he is confronted with a long list of 'faults' in the kitchens. The inspector warns him that he will recommend immediate closure if the situation is not rectified within twenty-four hours. The staff, including the excitable, well-meaning, but not too smart Spanish waiter, Manuel, begin desperate efforts to clean things up. It transpires that Manuel keeps a pet which he thinks is an exotic hamster, but he's been conned into buying a rat. He hides the animal away on the inspector's next visit, but it escapes and runs out of the kitchens into the dining room.

Egypt, 1983

Years before, on a trip to Egypt in 1983, I'd travelled by train from Cairo to Luxor further up the Nile. Walking from the station, I was looking for the guest house where I planned to stay for a few nights. I stopped to ask directions from a young man standing outside his house – no Google Maps or smartphones in those days. He invited me in for some tea and ushered me into a well-furnished living room. In a short while, he came back with a teapot, glasses, two plates of meat and a bowl of rice. As I scooped up a modest portion, I thought I saw some movement. Was I dizzy with heatstroke? I'd spent an uncomfortable day in bed with an attack in Cairo. On closer inspection, grains of rice were clearly moving. Disturbed by my spoon, the maggots wriggled vigorously. My host just shrugged as if it were normal. I thanked him for the tea and went on my way.

A few days later, I travelled by train to Aswan, the town furthest south on the Nile in Egypt. After a lazy afternoon sailing by felucca to Elephantine Island, I returned to Aswan. I was planning to take a steamer up the Nile to Wadi Halfa and from there travel south into Sudan. Unfortunately, the service was suspended because one of the two steamers had just sunk in Lake Aswan. I would have to find another way of getting to Khartoum when the chance came.

In May 1983, a steamer on the River Nile with about 600 passengers on board sank on a routine trip between Aswan and Wadi Halfa. The boat caught fire after a gas bottle exploded in the engine room, and it sank in the lake above the Aswan Dam. It was reported that 48 people died, 254 were missing, and 325 were rescued.

In the evening, when the temperature was more bearable, I walked along the riverbank looking at the boats moored there. I met a young American woman who was travelling on her own in Egypt. We went for dinner on a floating restaurant, an old wooden houseboat. We swapped travellers' tales and were relieved that none of the local food we ordered showed signs of moving on the plate Melissa had been having a difficult time dealing with unwanted attention from young Egyptian men who seemed to think all Western women in Egypt were there just to have a fling with an Arab man. She was even more scathing of her compatriots who had come with that in mind, making life difficult for other women who just wanted to travel independently.

India, 1970

Independent budget travel in Asia at the beginning of the 1970s was a journey back in time. With no Lonely Planet guides, internet or mobile phones, it was difficult to book in advance for cheap accommodation and transport, and information was often passed on by word of mouth. Taking the cheap options meant paying in terms of discomfort and harassment. Young Westerners could be subjected to irritating and childish provocation by bored passengers on a long journey. This was particularly the case when travelling third class on crowded trains in India, and on trains in eastern Turkey, where groups of young men were leaving to work in Germany. To escape being pestered on journeys of several hours on Indian trains, the best option was to climb onto the luggage shelf. It was wide enough to lie down there above the seething mass of people pushing and shoving to get in and out at stations, climbing in through windows, jostling for space, and sitting on the floor.

Calcutta Streets

To reach India from Thailand in 1970, it was necessary to fly as the border with Burma had been closed. Short-stay visas allowed a stopover in Rangoon (Yangon) for those on a flight from Bangkok to Calcutta (Kolkata). I spent two humid nights in the city visiting colourful markets, eating at street stalls, and walking around the golden Shwedagon Pagoda built in the time of the Buddha. Arriving in the chaos of Calcutta after a restful couple of days in Rangoon was something of a culture shock. I shared an old yellow Ambassador taxi from Dum Dum airport to the Chowringhee district and found a budget hotel in a dingy alleyway at the back of Sudder Street. I'd heard of it on the grapevine, and at 2 US$ for a twin-bed room with a cold shower and a hole in the floor toilet, it was certainly cheap. Opening the shutters of the small window, I could see across the narrow alleyway into the courtyard of the house opposite. A bearded man in a white singlet and dhoti emerged through the gateway, whose stone pillars were covered in graffiti. Much of the writing was in Bangla script, but English words proclaimed that a 'Charter of Demand' must be settled immediately. There was a strong radical tradition in Calcutta, and one of the trade unions was demanding a minimum wage and workers' rights.

On the way to Chowringhi from the airport, it became clear that thousands of people were living in poverty far more dire than any I'd seen in south-east Asia. Better-off citizens could afford one of the many horse-drawn carriages to take them along congested streets like those shown in old photographs of Edwardian London. Two-wheeled cycle rickshaws were also common, but the cheapest were hand-drawn. A thin barefoot rickshaw wallah strained to maintain momentum, pulling on two parallel bars to haul a far heavier man along through slow-moving traffic. This seemed to epitomise the degrading working conditions of the poor as it did in the days of the British Raj and the East India Company.

In the evening, I walked through the dark streets to a busy road teeming with cycle rickshaws. Overloaded double-decker buses with young men clinging to the outside somehow made their way along. On the pavement, street vendors prepared samosas and snacks for passers-by with a few rupees to spend. Mothers cooked vegetables and chapattis on small kerosene stoves, eagerly watched by their children. Further along, I stepped over the outstretched legs of people lying on the pavement amidst the bustle and noise, with nowhere else to go. Whole families sleeping out there, hundreds displaced by floods from homes in West Bengal. With few functioning street lights, the kerosene lamps of vendors cast moving shadows of passers-by onto the walls, flitting along like dark ghosts fleeing the hubbub.

The following morning, after a sound sleep in the surprisingly quiet room at the back of busy Sudder Street, I sat on a low stool on the pavement to eat a breakfast of fried eggs, chapattis and tea. A barefoot labourer wearing an old sarong pulled a hand-cart piled with vegetables for the market. Two men pushed a heavier wooden cart along, loaded with household furniture. People were striving to make a living amidst deprivation and destitution. Later, I crossed the Hooghly River on Howrah Bridge, where a human tide flowed in both directions. That energy was there in the crowded streets of Dhaka, the capital of Bangladesh, where I lived years later. Millions of Bengalis were just about making a living driving cycle rickshaws, labouring, working in clothes factories, or street trading, many with only a shanty dwelling of sticks and plastic sheeting to keep the rain off at night.

Nepal, 1970, 1973

Health for All

Bouts of fever and diarrhoea were common in the unhygienic and insanitary conditions prevalent in the crowded towns and cities of India in the early 1970s. The poor had little knowledge about how to prevent disease or the resources to improve their living conditions. The World Health Organisation's aim of health for all at all ages was a distant goal but above question. After visiting India and Nepal in 1970 on my way back to England from Australia, I travelled back on trains and buses in 1973. Soon after arriving in Kathmandu, I experienced a mild fever. Bouts of fever lasting a day or so were nothing unusual on the sub-continent, and I had no problem travelling around for a few weeks before returning to England overland. Through the winter, I experienced backache and lethargy, but was not aware that I had a malaria infection. The typically severe symptoms were suppressed when I was abroad and taking chloroquine, and it was not widely known at the time that the parasite was becoming resistant.

The infectious disease malaria is caused by a protozoan parasite transmitted by the bite of an infected female Anopheles mosquito. The most common forms are Plasmodium falciparum malaria, which is often fatal, and Plasmodium vivax malaria, characterised by recurrent fever, high temperature, chills, shaking, headache and nausea. Recovery from an untreated infection can be followed by relapses when parasites emerge from isolation in the liver. The National Malaria Control Programme launched in India in 1953 dramatically reduced the number of reported cases by the mid-1960s, but after this initial success, there was a resurgence and resistance to chloroquine was reported in 1973. ...

England, 1974

...On returning to England in November 1973 after my second visit to India and Nepal, back pain disrupted my sleep, and this continued through the winter. I had no idea that malaria parasites were hibernating in my liver. When spring arrived in 1974, I had more energy and went to London to work. After a week or so, the aches and pains returned along with a fever. When these symptoms persisted, I went to the local surgery where a recently graduated male doctor diagnosed influenza. The symptoms became severe and debilitating in the next few days, and it was clearly something more serious. In the afternoons, there was some respite, so a few days later, I was able to get to the surgery again. Despite my description of the symptoms I was experiencing, the same doctor just said I was 'run down' and suggested I drink Coca-Cola! Over the next few days, vomiting and uncontrollable shaking in the mornings prevented me from keeping food down. At night, I woke up sweating and shaking violently. One night, the wall by my bed seemed to ripple like a sheet on a washing line.

In those days, primary care under the National Health Service allowed sick people to visit a local surgery and wait in turn to see a doctor without an appointment. I realised that I had to be proactive if I saw the same doctor, and I insisted he refer me to the hospital for a blood test. I managed to walk slowly to the major teaching hospital about half a mile away, but struggled on the way back, having to stop several times to rest. When I reached home exhausted, the doctor was there, waiting with his car to take me back to the hospital straight away. The blood test had revealed many *P. vivax* parasites, but there were few red blood cells left. That night, I sweated profusely on rubber sheets in a hospital bed, my temperature higher than I thought possible. The fever magnified a noise like racing cars going up through the gears, and I thought I was lying beside the Silverstone race track. By morning, quinine had quelled the fever, and I realised there were cars accelerating away from traffic lights in the street below.

Nepal, 1970

Three years earlier, in 1970, chloroquine had been very effective for the prevention of malaria when I travelled back to England overland from Australia. In densely populated Calcutta, I walked across the crowded Howrah Bridge over the Hooghly River. At the station on the other side, I bought a ticket for a train to Patna that would leave the next day. From there, I crossed the Ganges on a bus that took me north up to Raxaul. In the mellow morning light just after dawn, I took a horse-drawn buggy to the border with Nepal.

Distant Peak

After a few days exploring the crowded streets and alleyways in the old part of Kathmandu, I took a short bus ride to the former capital, Bhaktapur, a much smaller town of temples and old red-brick tenements. I hiked all day across rice fields and up into the hills around Nagarkot. From there on a clear morning in winter, there is a spectacular view of the Himalayas. Just after dawn the next day, on a typically crisp and bright January morning, I sat on a hillside looking out across the vast Kathmandu Valley. Awe-inspiring ice-capped mountains stretched right across my arc of vision. With a sketched profile of the peaks I'd found in a book shop, I was able to identify Mount Everest, Sagamartha, 150 kilometres away. At least, I convinced myself that a distinct 'M' shape on the distant skyline was the highest mountain in the world, next to its neighbour, Nuptse. I would have to take a closer look when I got the chance.

Tibet, 2000

Thirty years later, when I was working on health projects in Bangladesh for a few years, I flew to Kunming in China on vacation. From there, I travelled by bus to Chengdu and took a flight to Lhasa. The aim was to hike to Everest, Qomolangma, on the Tibetan side of the Himalayas. I arrived in Lhasa with altitude sickness and the worst headache of my life after the rapid ascent from 2,000 metres to more than 4,000. I spent the next couple of days strolling slowly around the town in some discomfort. When I felt fit enough, I bought a Chinese bicycle for a few dollars in the open-air market and cycled around Lhasa for a couple of days. When fully recovered, I cycled to a bus station on the edge of the city and found a bus that would go along the Friendship Highway towards Nepal. I hauled the bike onto the overloaded roof and sat down on one of the hard wooden seats inside. That night, I stayed in a guest house in Shegar, and after an exhilarating freewheel ride down the road for a mile or so in the morning, I found a truck that would take me to the rough track that eventually led to

Rongphu and Mount Everest. I climbed in the back with my bike, joining half a dozen Tibetans going home from the local market. Higher up on the plateau, there were signs of recent torrential rain, and a truck that had been coming in the other direction was stuck. It wasn't long before our truck was bogged down, and by late afternoon, it was clear it would go no further that day.

The road looked clear on the other side of the mud in which the trucks were stuck, and I could see a few scattered farmhouses in the distance. There was little prospect of sleep in the crowded truck, so I lifted my bike and backpack down and made my way around the deep mud to where I could walk along the road pushing the bike. After about half an hour, it began to get dark. I could see a faint light in the windows of a small farmhouse about a hundred metres away to the right. I headed down a track leading to it and knocked on the door. It was opened by a man and a woman who looked quite old but may have only been in their fifties. Not surprisingly, they appeared slightly nervous when they saw a tall foreigner standing outside. We had no common language, but they quickly understood I needed somewhere to sleep, perhaps by intuition rather than my mime of a truck getting stuck. The couple were clearly poor and accepted my offer of some money. After a meal of hot stew and flat Tibetan bread, my hosts were more relaxed and brought some rough yak-wool blankets and a mat so I could sleep on the floor.

Tibetan Plateau

The next morning, after a breakfast of yak-butter tea and bread, I set off in the fresh, rarefied air and bright sunlight. I could push the bike up gradual slopes and freewheel down long descents, which was what I had in mind when I bought it. The road wound down to a stream flanked by green pasture where a yak herd was grazing – an idyllic scene with white clouds billowing over rounded mountain tops, and snow peaks in the distance. My euphoria was shattered when the stem holding the saddle broke off. The combined weight of my 85 kilograms and heavy backpack was too much for a bike designed for smaller Chinese people. I had seen no other vehicles since leaving the mud, and most likely, the trucks were still blocking the road. I sat down to eat some dried fruit and bread and assess the situation.

The hollow stem that held the saddle had broken off where it fitted into the frame. It would have to be narrower to fit in again. After bashing the end of the stem with a stone for a while, I was able to jam it into the frame. Thinking this new arrangement wasn't going to last very long, I set off with my pack in the front basket, trying to keep my weight off the saddle. Standing on the pedals on downhill stretches and pushing the bike up the inclines worked reasonably well. For the most part, I made easier progress than if I'd been hiking all the way carrying a heavy backpack. Eventually, I reached the village of Chay, where I planned to stay the night before starting the hike to Everest across the foothills.

At the edge of the village, a man working on a small plot of land directed me to a nearby farmhouse when I mimed that I needed somewhere to sleep. Three generations of the family came out to give me a friendly welcome and showed me upstairs to the living area above the animal stalls. When I'd rested for a while, we all had dinner around the bare wooden table – delicious goat meat stew with freshly baked flat bread. The family left to sleep in another part of the house, and I stretched out on a wide bench along one side of the living room open to the mountain air. I was glad of the wool rugs I'd been given, and in the morning drank hot tea and ate warm Tibetan bread with some yoghurt. I had to set off early with a long walk ahead to the next place where I could stay. I used one of my few Tibetan words to say goodbye and gave the family my bicycle. I wasn't planning to come back the same way, and it could be repaired in the market where I'd boarded the truck. They pointed me in the direction of Qomolangma, Mount Everest, and the village with a tea house where I could stay that night. I had a compass, water, Tibetan bread, dried fruit and an exhilarating sense of freedom in an open and remote landscape.

Himalayan Foothills

I hiked up all morning to the Geu-la Pass, where the view towards the distant mountains was inspiring. In the afternoon, I stopped for a brief chat with three children herding goats. Their sun-browned faces were full of pride as they tried out a few of the English words they'd learnt in school. In four days crossing the foothills to Rongphu, I saw no other hikers, only Tibetan villagers in Tashi Dzom, Pasum and Cho Dzom, where I stayed in tea houses at night. I caught glimpses of Everest along the way, but when I reached Rongphu Monastery, Qomolangma was mostly obscured by cloud. It was only partly visible when I hiked for two hours to reach base camp at 5,200 metres the next morning. I would have to look at the Nepal side of the mountain when the chance came.

Only three other people were staying at the lodge in Rongphu, Chinese traders from Shigatze, who were going to drive down to Nepal to do some business. They accepted my offer to share fuel costs for what was then a two-day journey. The spectacular road wound down from 4,000 metres on the Tibetan plateau to the Kathmandu valley. One section was carved into the steep face of a mountain with waterfalls spilling overhead into a vast chasm and the ravine far below.

Nepal, 2001, 2002

I visited Nepal several times to go trekking in the mountains when I was living and working in Bangladesh. At the end of March 2001, I took the two-hour flight from Dhaka to Kathmandu and caught a bus from there to Pokhara to visit the Annapurna region. At over 8,000 metres, Annapurna is the highest mountain in a natural amphitheatre formed by several peaks over 7,000 metres known as the Annapurna Sanctuary. Sadly, my hike up to base camp was marred by an avalanche that killed four hikers. They were buried in a fall of ice and snow earlier that afternoon, a few hundred metres up from the lodge where I was going to stay the night. A young Israeli on his way down told me he'd reached the lodge just before the fall and was keen to get off the mountain. I carried on up to the lodge, where the mood was understandably sombre among the three hikers and the two Sherpas working there.

Avalanches are common in the Himalayas. There were several in the Annapurna region in 2014, and in April the following year, a strong earthquake (Mw 7.8) triggered an avalanche on Pumori Mountain near Everest. The force of the displaced air blew tents from Base Camp across the Khumbu Glacier, killing several climbers. The epicentre of the quake was about 150 miles away in the Ghorka region north-west of Kathmandu. Tremors caused widespread destruction in the city, in

Kathmandu Valley and in other areas of Nepal, and several thousand people were killed.

At the lodge where the avalanche had killed four people that afternoon, I spoke to the Sherpas who'd been searching for signs of life. They said no one could have survived, and a rescue helicopter would not come until morning as darkness was falling. Guests and Sherpas huddled around a wooden dining table with a small kerosene heater underneath. We discussed what happened and if it would be safe to hike the next day. The four who died were on their way down through a ravine, unfortunately, on the side that faced the sun. I asked the Sherpas if it would be safe to go up past the fall on the other side of the ravine. They said the snow above would not melt in the morning.

The next day, the others continued on their way down. I decided to carry on as the thought of going back was depressing, and there was nothing I could do to help at the lodge. It felt eerie going past the snowfall where people lay buried, and I hiked up through the ravine as quickly as I could. It soon widened into a gorge, and further up, there were spectacular views that lifted my spirits. By mid-afternoon, I reached the next lodge at 3,700 metres close to Machapuchare, the 'fish-tail' mountain. The following morning, the gradual ascent along a ridge was awe-inspiring with a vast chasm on the right. The rumble of avalanches echoed around the amphitheatre of high peaks to the left. Descending from Base Camp to the lodge on the same day was quite tiring, but time was limited before my return flight from Kathmandu to Dhaka. Trudging through snow in the fading light for the last few hundred metres was hard going, but the hot meal and company at Machapuchare lodge was welcome at the end of an exhausting day.

When I visited Nepal again the following year, 2002, there were restrictions on where foreigners could go in the mountains due to the ongoing civil war. Nepal had undergone a partial transition from an autocratic monarchy to a parliamentary democracy by the 1990s, but demands for political reform had increased through protests and strikes. When efforts to suppress the popular movement by force failed, the king lifted the ban on political parties and appointed an interim government. A new constitution was developed for a multi-party parliamentary system with a constitutional monarchy. In elections held in 1991, the Communist Party won 69 of the 205 seats and periodically had control in the 1990s with support from other parties. A militant breakaway faction, the Communist Party of Nepal (Maoist), was formed in 1994, which aimed to overthrow the monarchy and promote the interests of the rural poor. Armed conflict with police forces began in 1996 in several districts. During the civil war, which lasted another ten years, the government controlled the main towns and the capital, Kathmandu, while Maoist insurgents were active in the rural areas.

In June 2001, the king and many members of the royal family were killed at the palace, not by insurgents but reportedly by the crown prince himself, who died a few days later from self-inflicted wounds. The government and the Maoists declared a ceasefire, but peace talks failed and armed conflict resumed with greater ferocity in November 2001.

Landing at Lukla

In February 2002, the civil war was restricting access to parts of Nepal and Maoist rebels detonated a bomb near the airstrip at Lukla, where most people start their trek to Everest Base Camp. I'd already booked a flight to Kathmandu with the aim of hiking to Everest. When I arrived in the city a few weeks later, I learned that treks for tour groups had been cancelled, but flights to Lukla were expected to resume in the next few days. That was good news as I had planned to fly to Lukla and hike independently. It would be easier to get a ticket and find accommodation at lodges on the trail. The rebels had achieved a limited publicity objective, and with a stronger military presence at the airstrip, it seemed unlikely they would strike again in the near future.

The Lukla airstrip, 2,845 metres (9,334 feet) up in the Himalayan mountains, is notoriously dangerous and often closed because of high winds or cloud. There have been several crashes since the airstrip was built in 1964. A small aircraft specially designed for high-altitude airstrips crashed into a parked helicopter as it headed down the runway for take-off in April 2008. The same year, eighteen people died when a plane crashed while trying to land.

With only a few Nepalis and myself on board, the 30-seater plane took off from Kathmandu airport at dawn. After a short flight with spectacular views of the mountains, we saw the scattering of buildings that is Lukla, with some roofs painted red, green or blue. The location is dramatic with the airstrip sloping up on a plateau from a cliff edge high above a huge valley. As the plane flew in to land on the strip, it looked almost impossible for it to stop before the main body of the mountain, only 500 metres up the runway. A fellow passenger said philosophically that most planes do stop, and with much clapping and cheering from the Nepalis, the plane landed safely. Taking off would be even more exhilarating with just enough runway to gather speed and lift off at the edge of the cliff. It was reassuring that the return flight was unlikely to be overloaded. No one else on the inward flight was going to hike the trail, and very few people would be on their way down.

I spoke to the soldiers guarding the airstrip about security. They thought the rebels had left the area and would be unlikely to interfere with a foreigner on the way to the first lodge. The security situation seemed less of a threat than the possibility of altitude sickness higher up, and with caution, there was a good chance of avoiding serious symptoms.

Everest Trail

I decided to set off, with a self-imposed rule to stop or go down if I had a headache, and only continue up the next day if the headache had gone. The distance between lodges allows someone reasonably fit to reach Kala Pattar (Black Rock) above Base Camp in ten days, hiking up for about eight hours each day, apart from one day to acclimatise in Namche Bazaar, the highest settlement at 3,500 metres.

Because of the altitude at Lukla, there is 30% less oxygen, while on Kala Pattar at about 5,640 metres (18,500 feet), there is 50% less. The body requires several days to adapt, and the lack of oxygen at altitudes over 2,500 metres (8,200 feet) affects most people to some extent. Mild symptoms include headache, lethargy, dizziness, difficulty sleeping and loss of appetite. The heart and lungs have to work harder to compensate for the lack of oxygen, particularly during exercise, and this can cause acute mountain sickness and death. The rate of ascent is a critical factor, and acclimatisation is essential. [4]

After crossing a spectacular gorge and the raging waters of the Dudh Kosi on a narrow rope suspension bridge, I followed the trail up to Namche Bazaar. I stayed two nights at the house of a Sherpa, Tashi, who had climbed Everest (Sagamartha) more than once. Although guidebooks advise against hiking alone, he said Sherpas at the lodges would advise about conditions on the way. He confirmed that my basic equipment of a compass, a bottle of drinking water and a sleeping bag would be sufficient as blankets and food would be available at the lodges. On a day spent strolling around Namche to acclimatise, I felt transported back in time watching two yaks draw a wooden plough through the dark soil. The next day, I felt fit enough to set off along the trail carrying a few spare clothes in my backpack. I met no other hikers on the way to Everest but exchanged greetings with Sherpas who were guiding yaks loaded with supplies for the lodges, and porters carrying far greater loads than mine. The mountain scenery over the next few days, with glimpses of Everest in the distance, was even more dramatic than on the Tibetan side of the Himalayas.

At over 4,500 metres, I decided to stop early in the afternoon on two days because of a headache. Fortunately, it had cleared by morning, so I felt fit enough to carry on. I reached the highest lodge at Gorak Shep (5,160 metres; 16,930 feet) in late afternoon on the tenth day. I had just enough time and energy to scramble to the top of Kalar Pattar, about 480 metres (1,570 feet) higher up. From that deserted vantage point way above the Khumbu Glacier and Base Camp, Mount Everest had a majestic presence. The deep blue sky was full of brilliant stars that shone more brightly as the sun's light began to fade. It was time to clamber down, taking care not to turn an ankle.

I reached the lodge, where the warmth and convivial atmosphere in the heated communal room was welcoming. I chatted to the medic with a small group of French climbers and an American couple heading to Base Camp the next morning. I didn't have time to go with them as I had only a few days to get down to Kathmandu for my return flight to Dhaka. I needed to leave early the next morning and descend quickly over the next few days. I'd already felt the magnetic presence of Everest close by on Kalar Pattar and enjoyed a clear view that was denied at Base Camp in Tibet. After a welcome hot stew of yak meat and vegetables with freshly baked flat bread, I soon felt drowsy. Leaving the warmth, I returned to my small room in one of the huts where I burrowed into my sleeping bag, wearing most of my clothes. Under an extra yak-wool blanket, I soon fell asleep. Waking in the night, I reached for my bottle of drinking water — it was frozen solid.

Pakistan, 1992, 1993

A few years earlier, I'd driven to remote mountain valleys in northern Pakistan with a friend I was living with in Peshawar. Karen and I took short breaks from work in the Afghan refugee camps to visit Chitral, Swat and Kaghan.

There are various ethnic groups in the mountains of northern Pakistan with cultures very different from those elsewhere in the country. The people are thought to be descendants of migrants who settled hundreds of years ago. Many have green or strikingly blue eyes rather than brown. In the Chitral Valley, the Kalaish people celebrate life with music and dancing. The women wear colourful clothes and mix socially with men. They have resisted attempts by people further south to convert them to Islam with its more restrictive culture.

In 1993, we drove up to the frontier town of Gilgit on our way to Hunza near the border with China. At that time, the Karakoram Highway north of Gilgit was just a narrow, unsurfaced track with a dramatic drop on one side and little room to pass any oncoming trucks. Driving past Rakaposhi, an imposing mountain over 7,700 metres high, our trip came to an abrupt halt. A massive avalanche several metres deep had blocked the road. The snowfall up the mountain was littered with pine trees uprooted from the forested slopes, and the force of the airwave ahead of the avalanche had flattened trees further down in the valley. A truck driver said he'd radioed for a bulldozer but didn't know if people were buried.

Like other mountainous parts of northern Pakistan, the area north of Gilgit is prone to avalanches and landslides. In 1994, a landslide near Attabad in the Gojal region raised concerns for people living there. Several households were relocated in 2006 following a geological survey. In January 2010, a landslide killed twenty people and blocked a section of the Karakoram Highway. The fall formed a dam across the River Hunza, creating a lake. The rising water threatened two of the largest settlements in the Gojal valley. Thousands of people were cut off, and many further south would be killed if the dam burst. The landslide delayed completion of one of the transport corridors along the ancient Silk Road planned under China's Belt and Road Initiative. The corridor between Pakistan and China was finally restored in 2015 when a realigned section of the Karakoram Highway with five tunnels was opened.

Confronted with the snowfall across the road in 1993, we drove back to Gilgit, left the Toyota pick-up there and returned to the avalanche by minibus. A few people had already crossed the snowfall, so we scrambled over and found a minibus on the other side that was going up to Hunza. We reached the small mountain town of Karimabad, the region's capital, in late afternoon and stayed the night at a small guest house with a very basic room. The charpoy bed had a wooden frame with woven strands of rope to lie on, but no mattress. The 'bathroom' facilities consisted of a bucket of cold water and a hole in the floor.

The Aga Khan Foundation promoted development in Hunza, encouraging men and women to participate in the process of modernisation through education, acquiring skills, and contributing time and resources to improve the quality of life in the community. Most inhabitants of Hunza are Ismaili Muslims known for their tolerance of other cultures and beliefs. The Aga Khan was the spiritual leader of this sect, which diverged from other forms of Shia Islam 1,400 years ago. The 49th Imam, by hereditary succession, he was believed to be a direct descendant of one of the Prophet Muhammad's cousins. Ismaili social values embrace the pursuit of knowledge, pluralism and integration into the modern world. As elsewhere, more conservative Muslim leaders view secular change and pluralism as a threat to what they regard as the Islamic way of life.

Underground Tea

After the avalanche season, we returned to the area and drove further up the Karakoram Highway to the Gojal region. North of Karimabad, we hiked to the Passu and Batura Glaciers near the border with China. On the way to Gojal, the remote, unmade road followed the Hunza River through an increasingly rugged and spectacular landscape. At one point, we stopped for a walk on a flat plain with apricot and walnut trees and a few crops growing. Life would be exceptionally hard in the winter with the land frozen or covered in snow. A thin plume of smoke drifted up from the ground a short distance away, and a man came walking towards us. Greeting us in English, he introduced himself as the only teacher at the village school. The people of Hunza have a reputation for hospitality, and he invited us to his home for tea. He led us to a hole in the ground from which the smoke was rising, and we followed him down a ladder to his underground house. He boiled a kettle on a charcoal fire — the source of the smoke above ground.

The main living space was furnished with a sofa, wooden chairs and a table, with colourful woven carpets on the floor and alcoves at the side for sleeping. It had been his family's home for generations.

India 2002, 2012

Around Christmas time in Darjeeling in 2002, I rose early to watch dawn break on Kanchenjunga across the valley. As the only guest in an old colonial hotel, I found myself outnumbered by waiters in the dining room that evening. After the meal, I asked one if I could have some tea. He came back surprisingly quickly, carrying a tray. On it was an unopened packet of Darjeeling tea.

In the small town of Pushkar in Rajasthan, Hindu pilgrims climb up to a hilltop temple overlooking a tranquil lake. After a hot afternoon doing the same in 2012, I climbed a wooden stairway to a restaurant in a narrow back street. The dining room was small with basic wooden furniture, but the atmosphere was warm and friendly. Ordering some curry dishes, I was pleased to hear I could get a cold beer despite restrictions on alcohol. After a while, the waiter arrived with a few plates of food, then returned to the kitchen. He came back with a large teapot and a glass. Thinking he must have misunderstood, I poured from the pot and took a sip – it was cold beer.

Pakistan, 1992, 1993

On a chaotic Pakistan Airways flight from Peshawar to Dubai in the United Arab Emirates in 1992, the plane was full. Many passengers wearing beautifully washed white jellabiya and turbans were peasant farmers from remote rural areas in North West Frontier Province. They had probably saved for years to make a once-in-a-lifetime pilgrimage to Mecca in Saudi Arabia for the Hajj. There was none of the rowdy antisocial behaviour sometimes seen on European flights. Islam does not allow the consumption of alcohol. Several passengers, possibly unaware of in-flight services, fired up kerosene stoves in the gangway to make a quick brew in mid-flight.

Tea in Karachi

Before the trip to Hunza, just after New Year in January 1993, I was asked to go to Somalia to work there for three weeks. Between connecting flights in Karachi, there was time to walk around the large open-air bazaar and sit down at a tea stall for some refreshment. The bearded stall-holder in a white jellabiya spoke some English, and we exchanged a few words about Karachi and what I was doing there. I told him I was living in Peshawar working on a health programme, and was on my way to Nairobi. From there, I would fly to Baidoa in Somalia and work there for a few weeks. He boiled a small kettle of water, then mixed in the tea and let it brew for a while. Holding the kettle high above the table, he ritualistically poured an arc of tea into a glass without spilling a drop. When I got up to leave, I held out a few rupees for the tea, but he waved them aside, saying, "Allah hafiz," – God protect you.

Somalia, 1993

The clan-based opposition groups that had overthrown President Siad Barre in January 1991 competed for power in Somalia. Heavily armed groups controlled different parts of the country in the absence of a central government. The political chaos, destruction of infrastructure, deteriorating security situation, and widespread banditry and looting exacerbated severe food shortages and hampered relief efforts. In November 1992, the United States offered to organise a military intervention to ensure humanitarian assistance could be delivered, and in December 1992, the United Nations Security Council authorised 'all necessary means'. The operation code-named 'Restore Hope' began a week later when US forces led a Unified Task Force (UNITAF) consisting of units from several countries, which invaded Mogadishu and other parts of Somalia. US Marines established a base in Baidoa to secure a protected zone for relief operations. Rebel militia retreated into the surrounding area, where they stole food from villages and made normal life impossible. Many villagers fled to the town seeking food and safety, but despite the military presence, there were militia attacks on relief agency vehicles and compounds.

After the flight from Peshawar to Karachi, I caught my connecting flight to Nairobi. I would fly from there to Baidoa and spend three weeks carrying out a health assessment of displaced people and reviewing the health services provided by relief agencies. The town is about 250 kilometres inland from Mogadishu, and the situation in the area, as in much of southern Somalia, was anarchic. Australian troops were due to replace the US Marines in Baidoa on 19 January 1993, and I was booked on a UN flight from Nairobi to Baidoa that would go the day after. The night before the flight, I stayed in Nairobi with Bart, an NGO colleague who was in radio contact with Baidoa. It was essential to get an update on the situation before going there. There had been no militia attacks on relief agencies in the last few days, so things were no worse than when I agreed to do the job and left Peshawar. It was time to control my nerves and get some sleep. Just after dawn the next morning, we drove to the military airfield in Nairobi. I climbed into the empty cargo hold of an old Hercules transporter plane, the only one on board apart from two Canadian pilots.

Landing in Somalia

After a noisy couple of hours, the plane landed on a dirt strip just outside Baidoa. I climbed down, waving goodbye to the pilots way above me in the cockpit. Looking around, I could see semi-desert with patches of scrub, but no buildings – there were none. There appeared to be a few trucks a couple of hundred metres away, so I set off to walk towards them. As I approached, it was a relief to see that the men loading the trucks with equipment and supplies from stacks on the ground were soldiers in uniform, not Somali militia. The khaki hats were distinctive - the Australian replacement force had arrived. "G'day," I said, reaching the nearest group. "I've come to do a survey of displaced people. Any chance of a ride into town?" A pick-up truck was about to leave with a few soldiers in the back, so I climbed in.

The truck sped off along a dirt track with a cloud of dust billowing out behind. In a kilometre or so, we came to the edge of town, passing several shell-damaged buildings, piles of rubble and a few burned-out cars. There were no other motorised vehicles around, just a few donkey carts with large metal drums on the back. Groups of men and women gathered around them, waiting to fill cans with water or kerosene. It was already quite hot when the Australians dropped me off at my NGO's compound. I spent most of the day there getting briefed on the situation in the area, and in the morning, met the young Somali teacher who would be my translator on the survey. Accommodation in the compound was getting crowded, so in the afternoon I went by car with two other expatriate colleagues to a newly rented house at the edge of town. On the way, I sat next to our guard, who poked his rifle through the open window to deter attackers – he looked no more than sixteen years old.

Guarded House

My room in the new house was adequate with a large bed, a wooden chair and a small table. It had bare plaster walls and wooden window shutters, which I could leave open at night for ventilation. I met the three young Somalis who would work in shifts to guard the house armed with rifles. They had mattresses for sleeping in the courtyard, which was surrounded by a brick wall about two metres high. A large metal-plated gate opened onto a dusty lane at the side of the house behind my room. It reminded me of the house down a dusty lane in Peshawar. Just before going to bed, I heard a deep rumbling sound coming from outside. Stepping out of the front door, I saw a small tank trundling slowly along the lane past the side of the house. The Australians may have started patrols, although I didn't see the vehicle again during my stay.

With little disturbance in what seemed to be a quiet neighbourhood, I soon fell asleep. In the night, a sharp crack of gunfire jolted me awake. The sound of several shots close by came from the courtyard behind my room, and bullets were hitting the house. Jumping out of bed, I pressed myself against the wall beside the window. It seemed the best place to be if bullets came through. The crack of gunfire was so loud it seemed to physically punch my stomach. My heart was pounding, but my head stayed surprisingly calm as I tried to assess the prospects if our guards were shot. The door to my room was locked, but I would have to bolt the window shutters as soon as the shooting stopped.

My ears were humming, but still on high alert when silence came, possibly a minute or so after the shooting began. I stayed pressed against the wall, not knowing what the outcome was. A voice outside shouted: "It's OK." I moved cautiously to the window and saw one of our guards in the courtyard a few metres away. He said two guys had been shooting at the house from the lane, but they'd run off after an exchange of fire. I joined the others in the living room and we radioed the main compound. Colleagues there were unable to contact the Australian patrol. It wasn't safe to drive after dark, so it was clear we had to stay the night in the house. One of the others thought we should all stay in one room until morning, but I said it was unlikely there would be another attack that night. I went to my own room, locked the door and the window shutters, and eventually got to sleep for a few hours after some deep breathing to calm my nerves.

The next morning, I went out into the courtyard to speak with the guards and thank them. I could see where chunks of masonry had been blown off the top of the wall from which they'd returned fire. A car arrived to take us to the main compound, where we discussed the security situation. I knew I had to decide whether to stay or get on the next UN flight back to Nairobi. Information about the displaced people was needed to arrange for appropriate resources to be sent. There were thought to be about 50-60,000 people living in makeshift shelters of sticks and plastic sheeting, but little was known about their health and demographics. Mothers and children would not have had access to health services for months, and armed militia had stolen food and animals from their villages. I discussed the situation with Jamal, my translator, briefing him about the information we needed, the way we would select a random sample of huts for interviews, and the questions he would have to translate.

Later that day, a young Somali lad drove us in a dilapidated old car to the camp at the edge of town to have a preliminary look. Two more lads sat in the back with their rifles poking out of the windows to warn off attackers. I decided to make a start the next day unless our informants heard of another imminent attack. Over the next two weeks, the survey went smoothly until the last afternoon, when Jamal came back late from his break, intoxicated. The town's weekly delivery of khat, a 'mild' narcotic, had just arrived. Fortunately, I didn't need him for more interviews, and we drove to the town's health facilities, where I interviewed the staff who spoke English and reviewed their records. A few days later, I faxed a report to head office on a satellite phone – there were no other phones, and no internet or email.

The UNITAF operation was considered a success under the mandate to protect the delivery of food and other humanitarian assistance, and thousands of lives were saved. However, the situation only remained stable while UN forces were present to deter fighting. Disarmament of rival factions within Somalia was not attempted, making a durable, secure environment difficult to achieve. There was a major change of policy with the transition to UNOSOM II in May 1993, as the new mandate for the multinational force included responsibility for nation-building. However, a national reconciliation conference aimed at forming a provisional government and numerous peace talks mediated by the UN failed. The UN began withdrawing its forces in December 1993, and all participating countries had withdrawn theirs by the end of March 1995.

Bosnia, 1995

'Sniper Alley'

During a cease-fire in a four-year siege of Sarajevo in October 1995, I flew there to spend three weeks analysing data from a health survey and checking details with those involved. I climbed down from the UN plane with half a dozen other passengers. Wearing heavy bullet-proof vests and helmets, we hurried across the tarmac to the damaged airport buildings. Forces of the Serbian Army were still occupying the hills from which they launched rocket attacks on the town. An armoured vehicle was waiting to take us into town along the infamous 'Sniper Alley.' As we bumped over potholes, I peered through a narrow slit in the thick metal plating and saw scenes of destruction. The boulevard was littered with bricks, rubble and chunks of concrete. Among the burned-out, shell-damaged tower blocks, some apartments appeared to be occupied, having washing hanging out to dry on the balconies.

The main route into Sarajevo from the airport is a wide boulevard which passes through the industrial area to the Old Town. During the siege of the city by Serbian forces from 1992–96, it came to be known as 'Sniper Alley.' Men with high-powered rifles and telescopic sights fired from nearby tower blocks, shooting to kill people going about their daily business for survival or providing essential services. Reports suggest that more than two hundred people were killed in this way, and more than a thousand were injured. No indictments were filed against individual perpetrators despite evidence available in military reports held by the UN International Criminal Tribunal in The Hague. However, one wartime commander in the Bosnian Serb Army, Stanislav Galic, was jailed for life by the tribunal for the terrorising of Sarajevo citizens during the siege.

The morning after I arrived in Sarajevo, I walked to Markale market in the old town. A rocket had landed there a few weeks earlier, killing several stallholders and shoppers. I passed the bridge where a Serbian nationalist had assassinated Archduke Ferdinand in 1914, triggering the Great War, and went to meet my Bosnian colleague Marko, who worked on the health survey. We visited his parents' apartment in a tower block in the old town, where they'd had a narrow escape. A shell fired from the hills had crashed through the back wall, the bedroom, and out through the front room window.

Australia, 2001

A few years later, surreal images of an airliner flying into a building were on my mind as my flight began its descent in Australia. It was a few weeks after the 9/11 attack on the World Trade Centre in New York in 2001. I was on my way to an international health conference at the World Trade Centre in Melbourne.

United States, 1972

In my restless 'odyssey years' I'd flown to New York from London, hitch-hiked across Canada, and travelled down the Pacific coast to Mexico and back to Boston in the east. On that three-month trip in the summer of 1972, I saw no violence despite staying in some big cities – New York, Chicago and Los Angeles. This seems remarkable now as there is little control on people carrying guns, and police have shot several unarmed black Americans with impunity in recent years. 'Mass shootings' are common, and many victims are children.

Gun Culture

A mass murder in Texas on 24 May 2022 was the 27th school shooting in the US that year. Despite millions of Americans demanding more effective gun control, mainly white rural states with relatively few voters can veto changes in the law. Every state has two senators, regardless of its population size. National Vital Statistics Reports show that the annual number of deaths from firearms in the United States increased in recent years, from about 30,000 in 2005 to nearly 40,000 in 2017. Between 1968–2017, there were 1.5 million deaths in the country caused by people firing guns, including homicides, suicides and accidents. More civilians died from gunshots in that period than soldiers died in all US conflicts since the War for Independence in 1775. In 2020, more than 45,000 Americans died from gunshot wounds, the highest number on record. It had become the leading cause of death among children aged 1–18 years. [5]

On my overland trip in 1972, I experienced only two incidents of anti-social behaviour. I travelled down the west coast by car with two young Americans from Boston I'd met in Oregon. We visited a friend of theirs living on a commune out in the sticks. It was a warm night with a clear sky, and two of us slept out in the fields. Early the next morning, we were woken by the drone of a small plane which swooped down and sprayed - "God-damn hippies". More threatening was an incident in a small town in Texas where I was invited to stay the night at someone's house. In the evening, we went next door to meet a few young people from the neighbourhood. As I sat chatting to a young woman next to me about travelling in the States, I glanced across the room and saw a young guy pointing a rifle at me. Guns speak louder than Americans, so I said, "Good night, folks," and left for the quieter house next door.

Pakistan, 1973

The following summer in 1973, I travelled overland back to India and Nepal, not through Afghanistan that time – it was closed to foreigners after a recent coup.

In July 1973, King Zahir Shah, who had ruled Afghanistan since 1933, was deposed in a virtually bloodless coup by his cousin, the former Prime Minister Prince Daoud Khan. With support from military officers and civil servants, Khan abolished the constitution and declared Afghanistan a republic with himself as president.

I travelled through Iran on relatively modern buses along the western fringe of the Kavir Desert to Kerman and Zahedan. One evening, the hot air and curvature of the Earth's atmosphere magnified the setting sun, a shimmering red globe on the horizon. This very special image was balanced by a pink Persian moon almost as big on the eastern horizon as the sun began to set in the west.

I crossed into Pakistan at Taftan and boarded a rickety old bus bound for Quetta, 600 kilometres away across the Balochistan desert. Later that evening, the bus stopped in a caravanserai compound. Freshly baked naan bread and goat meat provided an unexpected supplement to my supply of biscuits and dried fruit. When the bus headed off again across the loose earth and sand, it was already dark, and the headlights revealed no sign of a proper road or even vehicle tracks. A few hours later, the driver stopped the bus, switched off the engine, and everyone else got down on the sand to pray. It was clear we would spend the night there. The Baloch and Pakistani passengers, who were mainly Pashtuns, had blankets and shawls to wrap up against the chill of the desert night.

The Baloch are an Iranian ethnic group mostly living in Iran, Afghanistan, and the Pakistani province of Balochistan. Competition between the many tribes has inhibited the development of a nation-state. Their ancestors are thought to have come from Haleb, now Aleppo, in Syria. They are mostly Sunni Muslims and claim descent from one of the Prophet Muhammad's uncles who settled there. Pashtuns (Pathans) are also an Iranian ethnic group of mostly Sunni Muslims indigenous to the region known as Pashtunistan in the south and east of Afghanistan and in the border area of Pakistan between Peshawar and Quetta.

The sand was still warm from the heat of the day, but I was glad to have plenty of extra clothes to add a few layers as the night would be cold. I slept on and off until dawn, then got up to stretch my legs and wave my arms around while other passengers prayed again. Later that day, the bus veered north close to the unmarked border with Afghanistan. As night was falling, the driver stopped the bus, and three men dressed like Balochi tribesmen boarded carrying rifles. When one of them reached my seat by the gangway, he waved his gun, indicating that I should get off the bus. No one else was getting off, and I figured there was safety in numbers. I shook my head slowly, looked straight ahead and stayed in my seat. He went by poking into people's belongings and into bags on the overhead racks, possibly checking for smuggled goods or guns. It was a relief when the three of them got down and the bus set off again through the desert night to Quetta.

Sudan 1989, 1990

In the semi-desert of north-eastern Sudan near the border with Eritrea, camels and donkeys were the main means of transport, with an occasional bus from Gedaref or Kassala.

The Rashaida, a tribe of Bedouin Arabs originally from the Saudi peninsula, lead a traditional semi-nomadic way of life rearing camels and herding them to markets in that remote region. They had a more permanent tented camp and periodically held a camel market in Showak, where I lived for a year in 1989-90. This small settlement of thatched huts, mud houses and a few brick buildings is close to the Atbarah River, a source of water for goats and other livestock and a reliable source of dysentery for people in the area. I was working on health surveillance in support of the UNHCR relief programme in thirty refugee camps. About 900,000 people from Eritrea and Tigray were living there to escape the war in Ethiopia.

Civil war had disrupted life in Ethiopia since the 1960s, and many people sought refuge in eastern Sudan, particularly during the famine of 1984-85. The Eritrean People's Liberation Front (EPLF) signed a peace deal with the Ethiopian government in November 1989, but hostilities resumed. The Tigray People's Liberation Front (TPLF) led armed opposition to Mengistu's regime, which was overthrown in May 1991. A transitional government was established in Eritrea, which became an independent country after a referendum. The TPLF was dominant in a coalition of ethnically-based parties in a federal Ethiopian government, but was ousted in 2018 following widespread discontent with years of repression. It refused to join a new coalition, and in November 2020, there were military confrontations between Tigrayans and Ethiopian forces, which resulted in thousands of refugees crossing into eastern Sudan again.

The Rashaida were an exotic presence around Showak in 1989–90, the men wearing turbans, white robes and swords in leather sheaths, while the women wore black away from their camp. A narrow slit in their veils revealed feisty black eyes as I passed three young women coming from the marketplace. They giggled mischievously at the khawaja, the white foreigner, as he went by. A pick-up truck arrived from Gedaref carrying crates of Coca-Cola bottles chilled on blocks of ice. A group of young Rashaida men stood around in the sparsely stocked market, swigging from dusty bottles. News travelled fast on the 'grapevine' when a consignment was on the way – there were few 'treats' in town and they didn't last long.

In keeping with Muslim culture, alcohol was officially banned, although a bottle of Gordon's gin smuggled in through Port Sudan could be bought for a UN volunteer's monthly allowance. An alternative was illicit araqi, made from dates, which was sold at a more reasonable price by a black lady from the south in her small hut at the edge of town. It was illegal even before the Islamists gained control of the administration. When I went to the hut to buy a bottle, the town's policeman was sitting outside with a glass of firewater in his hand.

Breath Test

In that remote location, before the National Islamic Front (NIF) asserted its influence, drinking araqi was more a health risk than a serious transgression. Under the strict Islamist regime that followed, the penalty was several lashes and a hefty fine. The drink was not unpleasant, topped up with juice from big pink grapefruit that were sometimes available in the market. A large bottle occasionally livened up the conversation among a small group of expatriates who met in my compound on a Thursday night before the rest day. One of them was a young volunteer, a carpenter helping to build a new school. One Friday morning, he drove his old pick-up truck into one of the poles supporting electricity cables in the lane behind my hut. The accident might have gone unnoticed by local officials if the electricity supply hadn't failed. Although power cuts were common, the town's policeman decided to launch a full investigation. Jamie explained that he'd swerved on the sandy track to avoid a man on a camel coming towards him. His story was entirely plausible as the Rashaida often rode camels along the lane, and I'd once seen two having a race there. The policeman suspected alcohol was involved and insisted the driver take a breath test. He was escorted to the town's medical tent, where the local Sudanese doctor sat at his desk in a smart white coat. He rolled a newspaper up into a cone and told Jamie to blow into the narrow end. With a sniff at the other end, he pronounced, "He's not been drinking."

The thatched hut I lived in was made of rough sand-coloured bricks with walls about two metres high. It was rectangular rather than round like a traditional African tukel, with the room just big enough for a small chest of drawers and a double mattress on a raised stone platform. A metal armchair with cushions was comfortable for reading when there was electricity, or for sitting outside in the evening watching blue waxbills feed in a tree by the door. One evening as I sat by the doorway, big drops of rain exploded in the fine dust before a torrential downpour. A scorpion with its tail curled up scurried past my feet seeking shelter from the rapidly flooding compound. As it rested in a corner of the hut, a well-aimed boot ensured I would get to sleep that night. Hand-sized camel spiders were another hazard, and a search for them became a bedtime ritual after finding one in the top corner of the mosquito net.

Desert Fox

A surprisingly rich variety of wildlife flourished in the sparse vegetation of the surrounding area and in the arid terrain away from the river. One day, two Sudanese boys from a neighbouring hut brought me a young desert fox they'd caught, a handsome creature with soft cream-coloured fur. As they handed it over, it bit me. I'd been given preventive vaccinations against rabies in England, but needed a booster after the bite. It took several hours and three buses the next day to get to Khartoum hospital for an injection.

Military Coup

Life in Showak had been quite remote from the political developments in the capital. I hadn't been to Khartoum for nearly a year since I first arrived in Sudan in October 1989; my departure from England was delayed over the summer because of a military coup.

In June 1989, a Sudanese army force led by Brigadier Umar Hasan al-Bashir seized power and overthrew the elected civilian government. The coup followed growing confrontation between the army and the Prime Minister, Sadiq al-Mahdi. There were public demonstrations against economic hardship, and many people demanded the return of the former dictator al-Nimeiry, who had been in exile in Egypt since being ousted in 1985. Al-Bashir declared himself Head of State, Commander in Chief, Defence Minister and Prime Minister. Parliament was dissolved, and a military junta ruled the country.

Dangerous Dogs

Emergency measures, including an overnight curfew, were still in force when I first arrived in Khartoum in 1989, a few weeks after the military junta took control. The situation seemed stable, although on the first night, my roommate and I heard gunshots in the street below the window of our hotel room on the first floor. We lay down below the window until the shooting stopped a few minutes later. Tired after a long flight, I went to bed and fell asleep. The next morning, hotel staff told us the police had been shooting stray dogs, which sounded plausible as there were many roaming the streets in packs. Walking around town and in the bazaar in the daytime, local people were friendly and hospitable towards foreigners.

General al-Bashir's military regime had little popular support among the mainly Arab population in northern Sudan, who were not used to ruthless repression. He introduced harsh measures to control educated elites who, in the past, had supported popular uprisings. The Revolutionary Command Council imprisoned hundreds of political opponents, banned trade unions and political parties, silenced the press, and dismantled the judiciary.

When I returned to Showak after the rabies injection in Khartoum in 1990, the military regime had been in power for over a year. Some senior Sudanese colleagues were already expressing support for an Islamist agenda. I was due some leave after working for nearly a year, and booked a flight to Addis Ababa in Ethiopia. I would spend a few days there before flying to Kenya for a two-week vacation in August. There was relative calm in the small departure lounge after an unruly scrum at the only check-in desk. As I waited, a Sudan Airways plane could be seen coming in to land, and several people hurriedly gathered up their belongings and left to board the plane. It wasn't clear where it had come from or where it was going, but it took off a few minutes later without picking up passengers. Overbooking on the airline was common, and it was known locally as Inshallah Airways – Inshallah means God Willing.

Like most expatriates, I used other airlines and had no problem with my flight to Ethiopia. I spent three days in the capital, Addis Ababa, mostly exploring the vast, crowded and colourful open-air market, Addis Mercato, and hiking around the crater lake at Debre Zeit. After two weeks in Kenya, I returned to the more intense heat of late August in Sudan. At the immigration desk in Khartoum airport, the reception was noticeably cooler than when I'd first arrived in the country. I learned later that some expatriates returning from vacation around that time were denied entry by officious Islamists. The political situation and social climate had changed dramatically over the course of a year. A few weeks later, the voluntary organisation that had arranged my job with the UN-Sudan refugee programme withdrew its expatriates from the country. It would not have the resources to evacuate everyone from remote areas in the event of an emergency.

A ruthless internal security force had kept al-Bashir in power, supported by the ultraconservative National Islamic Front led by Hasan-al-Turabi, the only political party allowed. The Islamists reintroduced Islamic law, corporal punishment, and hudud, the amputation of hands and feet for theft. In southern Sudan, opposition to Shari'a law being imposed on the mostly non-Muslim population, and the unequal allocation of resources to the region, encouraged support for the Sudan People's Liberation Movement (SPLM). Under the al-Bashir-Islamist regime, the army continued a long-running civil war fought against the Sudan People's Liberation Army (SPLA), which had widespread support among the mainly black and Christian population in the south.

Kenya, 1993-1995

When I visited Kenya in 1990, it looked like a more progressive country to work in than the Islamist state that Sudan had become. After I left Sudan, I worked on health surveys and surveillance in the Afghan refugee camps in Pakistan for two years, then welcomed the offer of a job based in Nairobi supporting health research and surveys in southern Sudan and East Africa. Between field trips, there was time to visit national parks in Kenya, Tanzania and the Congo. Sharing a house with Karen, my companion on trips to the mountains in Pakistan, our first visitors were vervet monkeys from the forest at the back. At the weekend, sometimes, we heard them scampering across the flat roof in the morning. One squeezed through the bars on the window and helped itself to bananas from the fruit bowl.

Unwelcome Visitors

We'd been living there a few weeks when one of Karen's friends from work arranged to come for a chat in the evening. We had a night guard to keep an eye on the compound and open the gate for visitors, but when she arrived in her station wagon, he failed to respond quickly enough when the car horn sounded. Two guys with guns hijacked the car and drove off with her inside. Fortunately, they let her out when they were clear of the town, and she got home physically unharmed. Shortly after that, we moved to another house with a high wire fence around the front garden.

One evening, Karen and I were sitting at the table in our living room having dinner. The door from the kitchen suddenly burst open, and four men rushed in yelling, two of them waving machetes. One held a knife to my throat, threatening to kill me if I moved. He ordered me to take my sweater off, and used it to tie my arms behind my back. I was made to lie on the floor, gagged with a scarf. My heart pounding, I lay there for what seemed like hours, but may have been only one. The knife-man got angry if I looked up, threatening to kill me if they didn't find the safe – we didn't have a safe. Karen also had her hands tied and was made to show them where things were in the house. I felt powerless to do anything if she was attacked, but she stayed calm and showed them the US dollars we kept in a cupboard. When there was nothing more to loot, they began loading the TV, radio, cameras, clothes and other things into our NGO station wagon. There was a crashing of gears as they tried unsuccessfully to drive it away. The noise alerted the neighbours, who called the police – our phone line had been cut. By the time the police arrived, the gang had escaped on foot with all they could carry.

The level of criminal violence had been increasing in Kenya since the mid-1980s, particularly in Nairobi. Bank robbery, carjacking, housebreaking, and street muggings were common. In the early 1990s, the Structural Adjustment Programme (SAP), which was a condition for financial support from the World Bank and International Monetary Fund, began to have an adverse effect on living standards. Deregulation of commodity prices made essential items more expensive. Devaluation of the currency and a decline in demand for labour contributed to a fall in real incomes for the poor. The population of Nairobi almost doubled in the 1990s as people arrived from rural areas looking for work. Informal settlements grew rapidly, and the majority of Nairobi's population was crowded into relatively small areas of land with extremely deprived living conditions, and the urban unemployment rate increased.

The gang had cut a hole in the wire fence, tied up the guard and entered the house through the back door. We wondered if the guard was involved in some way, but he may just have gossiped in his shanty town about the foreigners he worked for and where they lived. I had flashbacks for months, visualising armed men bursting into the room. I imagined shooting them all, agonising over how I would have done that - futile thoughts as we had no gun in the house and I was tied up. Post-traumatic stress had only recently been documented as a medical condition. Walking in town, I saw men who looked familiar, but I couldn't be sure they were members of the gang. There was some psychological relief a few weeks later when a Nairobi newspaper reported that four armed men raiding a house had been shot dead by police. No doubt there were other gangs around town, and armed robbery was so common the city was known as 'Nairobbery'.

Dangerous Animals

It was a few days after the robbery in Nairobi that I flew to Goma to support health surveillance among refugees who had arrived recently during the genocide in Rwanda. After I returned to Nairobi, Karen and I lived in the same house for another six months, enjoying lunch in the garden at the weekends with red kites swooping down to steal sandwiches. On our days off, we made trips to the national parks, particularly those nearby at Lake Naivasha and Lake Nakuru.

One weekend, driving along a track through the bush near Lake Nakuru, we stopped in a clearing to have a picnic lunch. As we sat on the grass at the back of my old Isuzu station wagon, a fully-grown male baboon leapt onto the roof. He sat looking disdainful – the king of the castle. I'd seen territorial baboons in Pakistan baring their teeth in anger and knew the enormous canines could rip us to pieces. By the look on his face, he felt completely in command. The back door was open and I realised he could get inside and run amok among the bags, clothes and other things. I had to shift the balance of power. A stout stick I used for walking in the bush was on the grass nearby. Reaching over for it, I stood up slowly, holding the stick behind me. Looking directly at the baboon from a few feet away, I suddenly waved the stick like a samurai sword and roared – aaaaarh! Fortunately, this worked, and he leapt down and ran off into the bushes. It was time to pack up and go before he came back.

Living in Kenya, we had other close encounters with wild animals. On one weekend trip, we pitched our tent in a recommended location just outside a wire fence surrounding a safari lodge by a river. The disadvantage of that relatively safe location was a lamp in the grounds of the lodge that shone on one side of the tent. Sometime after dark, I heard a noise like grass being torn up followed by loud munching. Something big was moving towards the tent grazing. I held my breath as the silhouette of a massive head appeared on the tent wall. Hippos look clumsy on land and graze at night. Somehow, the enormous vegetarian managed to avoid trampling on the tent, possibly oblivious to what was inside. More threatening was an equally close encounter while camping next to a Maasai homestead.

Maasai sleep in rectangular huts with a flat thatched roof and walls plastered with mud and cow dung. The huts are in a compound next to the boma, a corral surrounded by thorn bushes protecting their livestock from predators that roam the bush at night. Our tent was outside the boma and the compound. After dark, we heard lions growling a few feet away, one on either side of the tent. The sound resonated in the pit of my stomach, and I held my breath with my heart pounding. Moments later, we heard the sound of human voices getting closer, men talking loudly. The growling stopped, and we heard no more lions or humans that night. In the morning, a few young Maasai men came to greet us, laughing about the night before. They had left the compound to protect the cattle. Walking quickly towards the lions and talking loudly was enough to scare them away.

Hunting lions is an extremely dangerous rite of passage in Maasai culture. Warriors once traditionally fought a lion alone on the open plain with just a spear and shield. When the lion population began to decline in more recent times, the Maasai changed this custom, encouraging young warriors to face a lion in a small group rather than individually to reduce the number of lions killed. The Maasai eat meat from cows, sheep and goats but not from wild animals, and they understand the role of lions in the savannah ecology. As the human population increased in areas around the Mara-Serengeti reserve, the population of large wild animals decreased, and livestock encroached on protected land. Many Maasai have given up some of their grazing land to support wildlife conservation, but partnerships with tour operators have been less welcome.

Southern Sudan, 1993-1995

Flying into southern Sudan from the far north of Kenya in the early 1990s, we spotted animals running through the bush that looked like wild pigs. Jan, the pilot, took the plane down to a few hundred feet to get a closer look. It was a herd of elephants spooked by the sound of the engine. We'd taken off from Lokichogio and flown north-west across a region inaccessible from the north of Sudan due to the ongoing civil war.

Western Upper Nile (WUN) lies on an open flat plain of grassy savannah and permanent swamp. A long, hot, dry season is followed by a wet season from May to October, when much of the area is flooded. The civil war between the government of Sudan's Arab and African army and the culturally independent Nilotic people in the south of the country began in 1983, disrupting normal life there, preventing commerce, and destroying what little infrastructure there was, including the very basic health services.

Semi-nomadic Nuer and Dinka pastoralists cultivate a few crops near their villages in the wet season, but live mainly by rearing cattle. They take the animals to water in the dry season and go in search of food in a 'hunger season.' Traditionally, they move back and forth between cattle camps near water and the relatively dry areas around the villages, usually walking at night when it is cooler. They pass through areas with thorn trees, acacia and balanites, which are the habitat of sand flies that bite at night. One species, Phlebotomus orientalis, is the vector of the parasite Leishmania donavani that causes the infectious disease visceral leishmaniasis (VL). The resulting syndrome of fever, wasting and enlarged spleen or lymph glands is known as kala azar. An outbreak of VL near Jikany was thought to have been the result of the war increasing the movement of people and soldiers through areas where VL was endemic.

When medical personnel recognised visceral leishmaniasis in Western Upper Nile in 1988, Médicins sans Frontières (MSF-Holland) set up a treatment clinic in Ler in May 1989, and another in the village of Duar, 80 kilometres to the north in July 1990. The surrounding area of Western Upper Nile, about the size of the Netherlands, was controlled by the Sudan People's Liberation Army (SPLA). When people heard about the clinics, those with symptoms would walk or be carried through the bush for days to get there because VL is typically fatal without treatment. Initially, one expatriate doctor and a nurse worked at the clinic in Duar for weeks at a time. Living conditions were extremely basic, and the clinic was bombed by government planes from the north. Other health workers came in and out on the four-seater plane that brought supplies.

MSF-Holland staff, together with the Sudanese health auxiliaries they trained, treated about 19,000 patients for visceral leishmaniasis from 1989–95, mostly in Duar. In that period, the epidemic in Western Upper Nile disrupted family and community life, caused great suffering, and killed an estimated 100,000 people in a population of about 300,000. Treatment at the MSF clinics saved the lives of around 17,000 Nuer and Dinka people. [6]

Nuer Village

Based in Nairobi, I was fortunate to make a few visits to the clinic in Duar to collect data on the epidemic. The main hazard for me on short visits of about two weeks was mosquito bites, although long grass had to be avoided as snake bites were quite common, particularly among children. I slept in a tukel in the village, a typical round African hut made of grass, sticks and mud. Between the top of the mosquito net and the roof, a cotton sheet had been stretched across from wall to wall to prevent straw and dust falling onto the bed. One night, I woke to a crashing sound as something thrashed around above my head. The culprit was a monitor lizard about a metre long that had fallen through the thatched roof onto the sheet. Switching on my torch, I saw the impression its feet made on the sheet as it clambered across the flimsy 'trampoline'. Scrambling onto the mud wall, it smashed its way out through the straw roof.

On another visit, I'd finished my work and was looking forward to returning to Nairobi as soon as the NGO's four-seater plane arrived from Kenya. Jan would stop for fuel at the airstrip in Lokichogio before flying to Duar. When we heard on the radio that the plane was stuck in Loki with a mechanical problem, I resigned myself to staying a few more days in the village with nothing much to do. The only other transport in that area of southern Sudan was a small UN plane, which was due to call the day after next at Ler, the village 80 kilometres away where MSF had its other clinic. One of the local Sudanese medical aides, James, told me he was going to walk there with three other Nuer men from the village. They were leaving that evening to walk overnight, so I asked to go with them.

Overnight Walk

The semi-nomadic Nuer are used to walking relatively fast over long distances with no water. I filled a large bottle with filtered water to carry in my day pack. We set off from Duar in the cooler evening air just after sunset, and at their steady pace, the cluster of huts in the village was soon out of sight. Walking at night through the bush, there was enough starlight from the vast Milky Way to see and avoid patches of scrub and thorn bushes. During the night, we could hear hyenas howling not far away, but my Nuer companions weren't concerned. Being in a group and chatting loudly was expected to keep animals away. About midnight, we reached a small hut where we rested for a couple of hours before setting off again just before dawn. A few hours after sunrise, we had walked about 80 kilometres in seventeen hours. For me, the cluster of huts at the edge of the village was a very welcome sight.

As we passed the first few huts, I heard a small plane approaching from behind us. I thought it must be the UN plane arriving a day early, but couldn't possibly walk faster to be sure of catching it. As it flew overhead towards the dirt landing strip at the edge of the village, I saw the dolphin nose and blue stripe of Jan's plane. On reaching the clinic, he told me he'd finished the repairs quicker than expected and had already called at Duar that morning. Malesh – never mind – it was a memorable walk beneath the stars.

Bangladesh, 2002

Health interventions by non-government organisations (NGOs) make a major contribution to relief and development programmes. The activities are often beyond the capacity of government systems, and NGOs are able to pilot new approaches that can be scaled up if evaluation shows they are effective. My first job in Bangladesh from 1999–2002 involved monitoring several NGO health projects to assess whether progress was in line with objectives and funding conditions. Most of the projects were focused on improving reproductive health services for poor communities and on AIDS prevention. Senior officials in the Ministry of Health were initially in denial, claiming that AIDS would not be a problem in Bangladesh because it was a Muslim country, but social research was finding that risk behaviours were widespread. One of our NGO partners was conducting serological surveillance for HIV among people at high risk, while another had a leading role in raising awareness and conducting prevention activities among them. When prevention work was well underway, a visit was arranged for the chief medical officer from the UK Government Department funding the project to see for himself how things were going.

Unexpected Meeting

On the last evening with our visitor from London, we drove with the NGO's field officer to a backstreet building in a downtown area of Dhaka. We met the NGO fieldworkers and the sex workers there and discussed prevention of AIDS and the impact of the project. The NGO also did AIDS prevention work with street sex workers who operated at many sites in the enormous capital city. I'd visited some of the sites before with NGO staff to monitor project activities, and had also met sex workers in the upmarket area where I lived. Sometimes in the evening, when it wasn't too hot, I would walk down the main avenue from my apartment to some street stalls and small shops. At a street corner on the way, there were usually two or three 'girls' waiting for potential clients to call their mobile phone or stop by in a car. It was unusual for a white foreigner to walk there rather than drive in an air-conditioned car. There was usually some friendly banter between us when I went by, and I sometimes stopped for a chat.

On the evening of the medical officer's field trip, it was getting late, and we decided to round off the day by visiting one more site in a residential area where the NGO fieldworkers met with street sex workers, discussed AIDS and distributed condoms. We had driven around a lot in the dark, and I'd lost track of where we were in the city. Our driver stopped the car on an unlit street. I got out with the others and walked a few metres to a small group standing near the corner. A young woman came towards us and greeted me warmly – "Kemon achen? How are you? You usually walk when you come to see us!" I wasn't sure what impression that gave our visitor, but I was told he enjoyed his visit to the brothel.

South Africa, 2003

The work with NGOs led to a job providing technical support for a group of social and medical scientists researching ways to provide basic health services in poor rural communities. The research centre in Dhaka, the capital of Bangladesh, was one of several institutions in Asia and Africa with health surveillance sites collecting data to monitor the impact of interventions. An annual international workshop was due to be held at a research centre in Mtubatuba, KwaZulu-Natal Province, South Africa. One of our female researchers would represent us and participate in the exchange of information and experience. Unfortunately, a few days before her scheduled departure at the end of September 2003, her family decided against her going as some parts of South Africa had a growing reputation for crime and violence. None of the other researchers was available and willing to attend, so I decided to go myself because it was important we were represented. I emailed the organisers explaining the situation and sent details of my flights and expected time of arrival in Durban. We'd been informed that participants would be met at the airport, taken to a hotel for the night, then driven to the research centre the following morning.

I received confirmation that I should travel as planned, but got no further details about arrangements before I left Dhaka a few days later. All went well with a flight to Dubai, a one-night stopover, a flight to Johannesburg the next morning, and a connecting flight to Durban, which arrived on time in the evening. Unfortunately, there was no one at the airport to meet the flight, no message at the information desk, and no response when I called the Durban number of the host institute. I had no idea which hotel the workshop participants would be staying at, and assumed they would set off for the research centre early the next morning. By then, it was late evening, so I decided to find a hotel for the night and make my own way in the morning if I hadn't made contact with the organisers. I could most likely get a bus to a town called Richards Bay up the coast and go to Mtubatuba from there on local transport. I phoned the hotel nearest the bus station and confirmed they had a room.

I hadn't been to South Africa before, but knew from other African countries that the area around a bus station could be dangerous at night. The taxi pulled up in front of a hotel less than a hundred metres from the bus station in downtown Durban. At that time, there was metal plating on the door and strong bars over the windows, which was a bit concerning but at the same time reassuring. Fortunately, the door was opened quickly when I rang the bell, and the night receptionist confirmed they had a room. I paid the taxi driver, who seemed happy to be on his way and wished me good luck.

Warning

I left my bag in the room and walked across a dimly lit area to the bus station. I realised the ticket office might be closed, but there could be a timetable outside. In fact, the office was open and I was able to buy a ticket for a bus to Richards Bay that would leave at 8.30 the next morning. I was told there was a café on the upper floor where I could get a drink and a snack. Parts of the bus station were poorly lit, particularly on the stairway. As I was nearing the top, I heard a voice close behind me – "You're meat." It didn't sound threatening; most likely slang for someone out of place who might be seen as 'prey' walking there at night. A young man disappeared into the darkness at the top of the stairs. I abandoned the idea of tea and a sandwich and went back to the hotel.

After breakfast in the café the next morning, the outlook seemed more promising if a little uncertain. I bought food and drink for the three-hour journey up the east coast, and waited in a comfortable seat as the coach filled up before setting off on time. At the bus station in Richards Bay, I soon found a minibus that would take me most of the way to Mtubatuba. It filled up quickly with locals and set off when it was full. In a small rural town, I was directed along a dusty track to a bush-taxi park about 500 metres away. Walking in a straggling line of passengers and local women carrying heavier loads than mine on their heads, I reached the taxi park. Asking around, I soon found an already packed minibus, which set off for Mtubatuba as soon as I'd squeezed in.

The driver dropped me off on the main road in a semi-rural area with a sprawling settlement of wooden houses and a few modern buildings. Fortunately, the research centre was well-known for its health services and AIDS prevention work, and I soon got directions from one of the locals. At the reception in the main building, I told the receptionist I'd come for the workshop. One of the organisers came down to the foyer to meet me, most apologetic about the administrative oversight and somewhat shocked that I'd walked through areas where most whites wouldn't go in a car. The other delegates were just having lunch, so I had a quick wash and joined them, having only missed the preliminary morning session. After the workshop, I went back to Durban, this time by car. Before flying back to Bangladesh, I enjoyed a couple of nights in the comfortable hotel where I should have stayed on arrival. In the morning, I walked around downtown and talked to some locals who told me they wouldn't stop at a red traffic light at night for fear of being robbed. At North Beach that afternoon, I had a strenuous swim as a strong tide began to turn.

Thailand, 2004

The following year, back in Bangladesh, I was planning a trip to Rajasthan in India, but by December, when the time came to book flights, I was feeling in need of a more relaxing break from work. Living in Bangladesh, it was relatively easy to reach countries in south-east Asia for a short vacation with access to beautiful beaches. I took a flight to Phuket in Thailand to stay a few days over Christmas before going to one of the small, largely undeveloped islands off the coast. When I arrived in Phuket on Christmas Eve, I found a guest house on Patong Beach, not far from Chalong Pier, where I might get a boat. The room was only available for one night as they were booked up over Christmas and New Year.

I slept well, and in the morning found a small boat with an outboard motor that was going to the island of Koh Racha Yai, about 20 kilometres south of Phuket. It sounded like an ideal place for a relaxing week of hiking, snorkelling and sitting under a palm tree reading a book. At that time, there was little tourist development apart from a dive centre at Patok Beach and a small resort complex on the opposite side of the island. A few hundred metres inland from the wooden pier and the dive centre, I found a cluster of wooden bungalows for rent. In the evening, I enjoyed spicy Thai curry and a couple of cold beers for Christmas dinner at a small café on nearby Siam Beach.

The Beach

When I woke early the next morning, it was already very warm, so after breakfast at the bungalows, I headed down to the quiet, empty beach. After a few minutes swimming in the clear, warm water, I settled down on the sand higher up the beach to relax and read before having to retreat to the shade when the sun got too hot. What happened next changed many people's lives. A powerful force rolled my body over and over, and I struggled to get my head above water. I stumbled to my feet with the sea swirling around me and tried to make sense of what was happening. I'd been hit by a big wave. How could that be so far up the beach from the shoreline? Regaining my balance and standing up to my waist in water, I groped around for my bag, towel and book as they floated inland. I managed to retrieve them and wade to a large rock that was now mostly submerged. I climbed on top and sat trying to gather my thoughts as the sea swirled past me towards the trees that had been the backdrop to an idyllic beach. I could only think a freak 'spring tide' had caused a huge wave. After a few moments focused on sorting my things out, I looked up. The sea had gone. I hadn't noticed the water flow out, leaving glistening wet sand sloping out into the bay as far as the eye could see.

I stared in disbelief at where the sea had been. It was strange and disorienting. A lone figure stood further along the beach, just staring out over the wet sand in the bay. The scene was surreal, and I had a strong feeling I shouldn't be there, as if awake in a dream. Looking along the beach, I saw two people walking towards me. The young German couple had been having breakfast at a café behind the beach when a report came on the radio about an earthquake in the area. I said we should get off the beach straight away and began walking quickly towards the vegetation and palm trees. As I climbed over a ridge onto higher ground, the water surged in again. I looked back to check the others were following and saw them up to their thighs in water, wading towards the higher ground I'd reached. We strode quickly along the path through the forest that led to the bungalows. Looking back, I could see debris from smashed boats and demolished huts, all kinds of plastic and pieces of wood being swept along by the tide of water powering its way through the trees. At the bungalows, I was relieved to find they were well above the water line.

Quickly stuffing a few things into my day-pack, I set off to walk to the dive centre to find out what had happened in the next bay. As I looked down the track that led past a row of low-level apartments, another wave smashed into the concrete buildings just up the track from the pier. I watched a man high up in the cabin of a large mechanical digger trying to manoeuvre it in the water. He must have been working on some construction when the first wave struck. The only other people in sight were a few tourists on their balconies, anxiously looking down at the surging water a few metres below. They looked high enough to be safe, and I couldn't see anyone in immediate need of help. I thought the surges could get more violent and destructive as water slopped back and forth in the huge bowl that was the bay. Remembering stories of 100-foot waves in storms at sea, I felt a strong urge to get to higher ground.

The day before, I'd hiked in the afternoon through the forest to the highest point on the island, so I set off along the same track up the hill. In a clearing at the top, I met a group of Finnish people who'd been taken there by staff from the resort. They agreed it was best to stay up there for the day in case bigger waves struck. I settled down for a long wait and put my things out to dry. As I opened the pages of my soaking wet book, a dead fish fell out. About index finger length, it had been squashed flat between the pages of the book as I snatched it from the water. Quite biblical — we just needed some loaves. In the afternoon, I talked to some of the others about going down to the resort to find out what was happening elsewhere. A few of us set off, and it felt good to be making a positive move.

Entering the outdoor lounge of the resort hotel, the normality of the scene was strange — comfortable sofas, a bar and a TV. Even more bizarre were the pictures on the TV showing the tsunami and waves lashing into beach hotels in Phuket that morning, only a few miles away. How fortunate for me that the guest house I'd stayed at on Christmas Eve only had a room for one night — it was right on a beach where most buildings were destroyed. Ironic that I'd decided to go to Thailand for a relaxing holiday rather than face the hustle and bustle of India. My experience of the disaster was personal and localised, but the enormity of the catastrophe was becoming apparent. I tried to call my brother, who knew I'd gone to Phuket, but there was no phone or internet connection to England. The forest was eerie as I walked to my bungalow to stay the night there.

An earthquake under the Indian Ocean of magnitude Mw 9 struck around 8am local time on 26 December 2004, causing a tsunami that lasted seven hours. Some locations reported waves of 9 metres (30 feet) or more when they hit the shore. Successive waves caused massive destruction and at least 225,000 deaths in surrounding countries. In Thailand, more than 5,000 deaths were recorded, with a further 3,000 people missing and over 8,000 injured. An official estimate put the death toll in Indonesia at 200,000, and thousands of people died in Sri Lanka, India, and nine other countries. [7]

The next morning, I went back to the Finnish people's resort and eventually got a landline call through to England. The TV in the outside lounge was showing more video pictures taken on mobile phones when the tsunami struck Phuket and other places in Thailand. The Thai navy was organising the evacuation of people from the islands, and a frigate was expected to call at Koh Racha the next day. I went back to the beach where I'd been hit by the first wave and saw remnants of boats and wooden buildings scattered among the palm trees. There was no sign of the restaurant where I had dinner on Christmas Day, and all the small cafes along the beach had been swept away. The force of the water must have increased with successive surges as the large rock where I'd sat down on Siam Beach was no longer there. Concrete buildings at the dive centre had been smashed. Back at the bungalows, the owner said he would soon run out of food as no supplies would come for a few days, so I decided to leave as soon as I could. He knew at least one person from his village had died, and the mood was sombre among people waiting for the navy boat the next day. It was a relief when it arrived, and all those ready to leave were able to get on board.

As we sped towards Phuket, I sat next to a Thai man who said he'd had no news about his family there. On landing, a taxi driver drove me to the airport without asking for payment. I joined a short queue for a Thai Airways relief flight to Bangkok. Some people were in shock, and I spoke to a young German woman with bruises on her face and arms. She'd been separated from her friend on a beach in Phuket. We soon boarded, and only a few hours after leaving Koh Racha, I was in Bangkok. I took a taxi into town and found a room in a hotel I knew in Khao San. I'd first stayed in that crowded, lively area in 1969 and returned several times. Now the streets were strangely quiet with only a few people walking around, some looking distressed and disoriented. The next day, I took a taxi to the airport and found a Thai Airways desk where flight arrangements were being made for people affected by the tsunami. Within minutes with no queuing, I was allocated a seat on a Thai Airways flight to Dhaka that afternoon.

Strange Call

As usual at Christmas, many expats in Bangladesh had gone to Thailand or Sri Lanka on holiday, but no one I knew was reported missing. Colleagues who knew I'd gone to Phuket were concerned, and one called my mobile number the day after the tsunami. A woman answered, who was crying and speaking in Thai. He couldn't understand what she said, but recognised the language because his wife was from Thailand. It was strange as my phone with that number had been stolen in Dhaka a few weeks before I went away, and I hadn't taken one with me. I could only think the stolen phone had been bought by someone from the Thai community living in Dhaka. Fortunately, the technology wasn't too 'smart,' so the phone didn't contain personal information or my bank details.

Guatemala, 2011

When I'd left Bangladesh a few years later and returned to England, I was no longer working full-time. I was free to resume some independent health research, which could be done in my own time with data available there. I could also travel to places I'd not been able to visit because of work commitments, personal circumstances, or wars. Between 2009-2011, I visited all the countries in Central America except San Salvador. In March 2011, a few days after arriving back in England from a trip to Mexico, Guatemala, and Honduras, I received a call from my bank. I'd just got home from filling my car up with fuel at the usual service station near my apartment. The bank's computerised security system for monitoring transactions had triggered an alarm as my debit card was being used at much the same time for an unusually large purchase, not in England but in Honduras. Most likely, the card had been cloned. I'd generally avoided using ATMs in Central America but had to get local currency in the evening when I arrived by minibus in Panajachel on the shores of Lago de Atitlan in Guatemala. Fortunately, the fake card was not used until the transaction in Honduras, which was blocked by my bank. I'd been able to use my own card to make payments until I appeared to be in two places at once.

Syria, 2010

I'd planned to visit Syria in the spring after the trip to Central America, especially Aleppo, Palmyra and Damascus, once important staging posts on the ancient Silk Road linking China with the Mediterranean and Europe. I applied for a visa in advance in November 2010, but was disappointed to learn that my online request had been refused. When I phoned the embassy in London, I was not surprised to hear they would give no reason for rejecting my application. It was intriguing as I'd never had a visa application turned down before. Still keen to visit the country, I decided to try a different approach. A week or so later, I flew with a budget airline to Larnaca in Cyprus, then travelled by bus to Kyrenia on the north coast. Two days later, I caught the early morning ferry to Taşucu in Turkey and travelled on buses for two days to reach Antakya. Once known as Antioch, the city had been an important commercial centre on the ancient Silk Road. The next morning, I caught a bus to the nearest Syrian border crossing. Within half an hour, an immigration officer had made a phone call to Damascus and stamped a visa in my passport. Across the border, I caught a bus to Aleppo, and by late afternoon, I had a room in a small hotel in the old city. That evening, I walked to the Baron Hotel, a characterful colonial building where I enjoyed a cold beer in the wood-panelled bar.

I travelled around Syria on buses, meeting surprisingly few foreigners. Wandering around the magnificent Roman ruins outside the desert town of Palmyra, I met only an Australian couple on holiday from work in Oman. In Hama, famous for its ancient water wheels, and in the colourful Al-Hamidiyah souk in old Damascus, I saw very few tourists. In the more 'liberal' Mediterranean port town of Latakia, young Syrian women chatted with friends in an open-air cafe, none wearing a headscarf. From there, I went by minibus to the Turkish border and in Antakya boarded a long-distance overnight bus to Istanbul. Soon after arriving back in England in December 2010, there were reports of growing discontent with authoritarian regimes in Arab countries.

On 17 December 2010, a young street trader in Tunisia set fire to himself in protest against police harassment. His death triggered demonstrations against the oppressive regime, which culminated in the fall of President Ben Ali, who fled the country on 14 January 2011. Within days, there were demonstrations against repression and poverty in Egypt, and President Mubarak was forced to step down on 11 February, leaving the Army in control. On 6th March 2011, a 13-year-old boy was arrested in Daraa near the Syrian capital Damascus after the slogan, 'The people want the fall of the regime', appeared on a school wall. His family and the relatives of other arrested boys demonstrated for their release.

Many people were arbitrarily detained in Syria during initially peaceful protests, which grew with demands for the release of political prisoners and democratic reforms. Security forces reportedly opened fire on unarmed protesters, and several were killed. More people were shot by security forces at the Central Mosque on 23 March. Peaceful demonstrations against al-Assad's regime became more violent and rapidly escalated into an armed uprising. The bloody civil war, a decade-long multi-sided conflict, drew in neighbouring countries, with Russia providing military support for al-Assad's regime.

The UN estimated that 5.5 million people from a population of 23 million became refugees, and at least 6 million were displaced within Syria. More than 200,000 civilian deaths were documented between 2011—2020, and an estimated 250,000 combatants were killed. Many towns and cities were destroyed, including much of the ancient city of Aleppo, which was bombed by Russian planes and Syria's own air force during a siege that lasted four years.

Bosnia-Herzegovina, 1995, 2016

In the siege of Sarajevo from 1992—96 in the Bosnian War, residents endured shelling, great hardship and food shortages. When I visited during a ceasefire in 1995, people were growing vegetables on derelict urban sites to survive, and the market area was empty. On returning in September 2016, the streets and markets were full of people shopping. Stalls displayed colourful mounds of fresh fruit and vegetables, and many of the damaged apartment blocks in the old town had been renovated.

The military commander who led Bosnian Serb forces during the Bosnian War was convicted of genocide, war crimes, and crimes against humanity in 2017. The charges included terrorising the civilian population of Sarajevo from 1992−96, and the killing of more than 8,000 Muslim men and boys taken prisoner in Srebrenica in 1995. In 2021, the United Nations war crimes judges in The Hague upheld the life sentence for Ratko Mladic for his role in Europe's worst atrocities since World War Two.

On my way to Sarajevo by bus from Croatia in 2016, I stayed for two days in the historic town of Mostar, which had also been under siege in the 1990s.

Following the declaration of independence by Bosnia and Herzegovina and fighting between Bosnian Croats and Muslim Bosniaks, Croatian forces shelled the Muslim area of East Mostar, causing much destruction and many civilian deaths. Religious buildings, cultural institutions and bridges over the River Neretva were damaged or destroyed, and thousands of residents fled.

Twenty years after the Bosnian War, I enjoyed a traditional Turkish meal in the tranquil courtyard of an old restaurant in the medieval centre of East Mostar. The stone arch of the Ottoman bridge and many old buildings had been renovated. The tranquil Muslim area contrasted with the busy street cafes and bars just across the restored bridge.

England, 1965

Bosnia-Herzegovina, Croatia, Serbia, Slovenia, Montenegro, North Macedonia, and Kosovo constituted the Socialist Federal Republic of Yugoslavia, when I visited in the summer of 1965. Although not a one-party state, the United Kingdom was quite socialist at that time with controls on prices and incomes, state-run public services and industries, and a functioning health and welfare system. Bulgaria, a totalitarian communist state within the Soviet Union's sphere of influence, had just opened up its road border despite a thwarted coup against the party leadership that April. Travelling through Yugoslavia in an old Bedford van with a few friends from college, we reached Bourgas on the Black Sea coast of Bulgaria before heading south to Istanbul. Before the trip, the van was useful for visiting pubs around London in the days before breathalysers were in use. Painted on the side of the van was an outline sketch of the Black Sea shaped like a bison in a prehistoric cave painting. Above this crudely drawn map was the ironic inscription – Black Sea Expedition 1965. One evening, driving along the Strand looking for the road through to the Aldwych, I turned right too soon into a short cul-de-sac. The way through was blocked by a set of wrought iron gates. There was no time to reverse before a policeman approached the van, looking suspiciously at the side. Ignoring raucous comments from those in the back who hadn't seen him, he peered in through the open window, commenting drily, "You won't get to the Black Sea that way!"

Wales, 2016

In the days before satellite navigation technology, there was nothing to blame for a wrong turn except poor road signs or an out-of-date map. Even now, physical maps can sometimes be useful. Satnav failed to recognise the village I was looking for near Llantwit Major in South Wales in 2016. In that part of the Vale of Glamorgan, there are many small villages connected by a network of narrow country lanes. Not all road junctions had a signpost, so it was sometimes necessary to stop and check the right direction using a conventional map. I eventually found the village I was looking for and checked in at a guest house for a couple of days to explore the coast before heading back to England. Because of the confusing network of country lanes, I used satnav to get directions towards Cardiff and the road back to England. The 'left' and 'right' instructions seemed to take me in the right general direction until I passed a row of houses at the edge of a village and entered an unmade road.

No Direction Home

A few hundred metres further on, the road became a dirt track with a hedge to the left and a wire fence three metres high on the right. I had just realised that the fence was the border of an airfield when a helicopter appeared overhead, hovering about ten metres above the ground. With no room to turn, I drove on slowly, tracked by the helicopter until I reached some closed metal gates. Fortunately, there was room for a five-point turn. Driving back along the track with the helicopter hovering behind, I saw a station wagon coming towards me. I was just able to squeeze past the police patrol vehicle and raise my hand by way of apology. On a prohibited road beside a Ministry of Defence airfield, the rapid response to an intruder was impressive. In satnav's defence, there was probably a way through to the Cardiff-road before World War Two.

A large Ministry of Defence establishment near the village of St Athan in the Vale of Glamorgan was officially opened in September 1938. During World War Two, it was used for training air crews and ground personnel. A dummy airfield was built a few miles to the west with aircraft and buildings made of wood and cardboard. This was attacked and rebuilt a few times, while the actual airfield stayed hidden. In April 2019, it was transferred from military to civilian control and is now owned by the Welsh Government.

Southern Sudan, 1994

No Roads, No Maps, No Mortars

I'd used an early GPS system to navigate while carrying out a health survey in the Upper Nile province of southern Sudan in 1994. The civil war had disrupted agriculture, and at one stage in the dry 'hunger season', many pastoralists from remote villages in Nasir District had gone in search of food. Their journey of several days on foot took them to an area near Malakal affected by visceral leishmaniasis, which was unknown to them at that time and fatal without treatment. With a nurse, Tom and an interpreter, I travelled to villages to interview people about sickness and recent deaths and take blood samples to test for infection. We had use of a pick-up truck, the only vehicle in a rebel-held area twice the size of Wales. There were no roads and no maps, but we had a satellite navigation device, GPS coordinates for the villages, and a compass.

After a few days of visiting villages, we were due to return to base and radio Lokichogio in northern Kenya to ask for the next UN plane in the area to pick us up. Approaching our base village through the bush, we heard booms in the distance – clearly the sound of mortar fire. At the base, the rebel commander would not acknowledge there were explosions, although the sound was unmistakable. He made no mention of it when he radioed for a plane the next day. It might deter pilots from flying in with much-needed supplies. There was no mortar fire in the morning, so the plane landed and we flew back to Kenya.

Following an agreement with President al-Bashir in 2005, which ended the long civil war, South Sudan became an independent sovereign state in July 2011. However, war broke out in the new country in 2013 following a split between the Dinka president, Salva Kiir and the Nuer vice president, Riek Machar. By the time power-sharing was agreed in August 2018, an estimated 400,000 people had been killed, and about 4 million were displaced from their homes. Fighting continued in parts of the country, and people faced food insecurity as well as the ongoing visceral leishmaniasis epidemic.

Another Civil War

After decades of rule from Khartoum, favouring the largely nomadic Arab population over the sedentary African tribes in western Sudan, they rebelled against al-Bashir's government in 2003. He called for support from the Janjaweed, Arab militia notorious for stealing from African tribes in Darfur. In 2013, he created a paramilitary organisation, the Rapid Support Forces (RSF), under the control of the Janjaweed leader known as Hemedti. In 2019, they were called on to support the army when protests against al-Bashir intensified in Khartoum. With mass protests against his rule continuing, the Sudanese army removed him from office, and its head, General al-Burhan, formed a transitional government in collaboration with the democracy movement behind the protests. Hemedti became his deputy, General Dagalo. In February 2020, the ruling military council agreed to hand al-Bashir over to the International Criminal Court in The Hague to face charges of crimes against humanity in Darfur. In April 2023, he was transferred from prison to a military hospital, where he was reported to be suffering from heart problems.

Just before a scheduled transition to civilian rule in October 2021, the military council declared a state of emergency and ruthlessly suppressed civilian protests in Khartoum. It later resumed negotiations with civilian leaders, promising to transfer power in April 2023, but when the time came, it refused to concede power to a civilian authority unless it was elected. Tension increased between General al-Burhan and General Dagalo, particularly over the proposed integration of the RSF into the army and Dagalo's role. Armed conflict erupted on 15 April 2023 when RSF forces captured Merowe airport. The army responded with airstrikes, and fighting spread to other parts of the country, leading to hundreds of civilian casualties and a humanitarian disaster.

Sudan, 1990

When I left Sudan in October 1990, it had been under military rule since al-Bashir came to power in a coup in August 1989. His regime was strongly influenced by strict ultraconservative Muslims in the National Islamic Front. Many other Muslim leaders supported the popular movement that contributed to his downfall in 2019. Most Sudanese in the north are Sunni Muslims, many following Sufism, a form of Islamic mysticism. As devout Muslims, they observe the religious practices of praying five times a day, charity, fasting and pilgrimage. They seek a personal spiritual path through chanting, singing, music and dance – anathema to ultraconservative Islamists with stricter codes.

Face in the Crowd

The weekly Sufi ceremony in front of the tomb of Sheikh Hamid el Nil in Omdurman on a Friday afternoon is an inclusive event. When I attended in 1990, more than a hundred Sudanese generated positive energy and a convivial atmosphere. Male followers wearing white jellabiya and skull caps formed a wide circle, clapping and chanting to the rhythm of loud drums. Inside the ring, Sufi dancers in jade green robes spun around with arms outstretched as they whirled around the circle. This induced a trance-like state, although the face of one old devotee in the crowd suggested brain damage. I had no camera with me to take photographs of the spectacle — no mobile phones or selfies in those days. When I returned to Khartoum later that year to leave the country, I looked around the bazaar for a postcard of the dancing. I found one showing a Sufi dancer in green robes spinning past a crowd of Sudanese, mainly dressed in white. Among them was a tall European in a yellow T-shirt who looked familiar....it was me.

England, 1963

Familiar Face

Years before, when I'd just left school and started work in Norwich, I went with two flatmates to our local pub for a beer after dinner. Waiting for the drinks, I glanced around the crowded room and saw someone who looked familiar. "There's Jack Kennedy," I said, telling my companions where the presidential lookalike was standing. After a couple of beers, we went back to the flat to get ready for work the next day. We switched on the TV for the evening news — President Kennedy had been shot dead.

President John F. Kennedy was assassinated as he rode in a motorcade through downtown Dallas, Texas. About 12.30 pm local time on 22 November 1963, his open-top limousine was passing crowds near the Texas School Book Depository at Dealey Plaza when shots rang out. With wounds to the neck and head, Kennedy was pronounced dead at Parkland Memorial Hospital at 1 pm (7 pm UK time, GMT). To this day, there are conflicting accounts of the events and many conspiracy theories about who was behind the murder and why.

It is generally accepted that Lee Harvey Oswald, a new employee at the Book Depository, fired rifle shots from a sixth-floor window. He was arrested within two hours but died in custody at Dallas Police Headquarters two days later. He was shot at point-blank range in full view of the press and TV cameras by Jack Ruby, a Dallas nightclub owner who was immediately arrested and charged with murder. Although convicted and sentenced to death, the verdict was overturned on appeal, and Ruby died in prison in 1967 before facing a new trial. The official Warren Commission report in 1964 concluded that neither Oswald nor Ruby was part of any larger conspiracy, either domestic or international, to assassinate the president. This failed to dispel doubts about missing autopsy evidence and the trajectory of bullets that hit Kennedy. In 1978, the US House Select Committee on Assassinations concluded that he was probably assassinated as a result of a conspiracy, which may have involved organised crime. This conclusion and that of the Warren Commission continue to be disputed.

Nepal, 1970

The Third Eye

Associating a personal experience with a major historical event like the assassination of a president makes it more memorable. Coincidences are commonplace, but for some people, an experience is so unusual and unlikely that it seems to have special significance.

In Hinduism, the 'Third Eye' symbolises an opening to higher consciousness and the 'Mind's Eye'. Its physical location in the middle of the forehead, just above the brow, is supposedly linked with states of mind in which clairvoyance and precognition can occur.

Between two large eyes painted on a wooden door in the old part of Kathmandu was an oval shape just above the eyebrows — the 'Third Eye'. The right eye looked straight ahead, but the left eye, with a squint, seemed to follow an old woman goading a black cow along with a stick. A ragged man staggered by bent double beneath an enormous sack, one of thousands who looked like refugees from an earlier age in the crowded medieval streets in January 1970. Men in tattered sack-clothes with long tangled black hair came from Tibet, where the Chinese had invaded, denying people the right to self-determination.

People from many ethnic groups lived in the streets of old Kathmandu, while others from villages in the valley and surrounding mountains came to peddle their wares or seek enlightenment. A Hindu fortune teller with a 'Third Eye' painted on his forehead sat cross-legged on the ground, a sadhu, face painted ghostly white with ash, chanted soulfully. I sat in Durbar Square in the old part of the city, discussing eastern philosophy and the concept of the 'Third Eye' with Rob from Australia, who was staying at the same budget hotel. Aware that a passer-by had stopped and was standing over us, I glanced up to see a tall, professional-looking man, well-dressed in traditional Indian style. In the middle of his forehead, just above the brow, was a deep indentation, about the size of an empty eye socket.

Afghanistan, 1970

Two men in ragged jackets and once-white turbans rode donkeys down a dusty lane in Herat, Afghanistan, near the border with Iran. They goaded two more donkeys to plod along laden with heavy sacks. Bright early morning sunlight projected shadows on the mud walls of houses at the foot of an ancient fortress.

"For in and out, above, about, below, 'tis nothing but a magic shadow-show, play'd in a box whose candle is the sun, round which we phantom figures come and go."

[The Rubáiyát of Omar Khayyám] [8]

Foreign Intruders

I'd walked through the old town with Theo from Paris, who had the room next to mine in a budget hotel. The fortress Qala Iktyaruddin, known to Europeans as the Citadel of Alexander, has been rebuilt several times since his army invaded 2,300 years ago. Huge round turrets and grey walls rose high above a colossal mound of earth and stones. From its base beside the lane, we watched the donkeys disappear into the medieval maze of alleyways and sand-coloured houses. The silent fortress once again towered over an empty lane. Stones the size of golf balls bounced around us like giant hailstones. Local Afghan boys had the firepower to force the foreign intruders to retreat.

The British Imperial Army was driven out of Afghanistan in the war of 1839–42, and again at the end of the second Afghan War of 1878–80. In 1989, Muslim guerrilla fighters forced the Soviet army to withdraw after its nine-year occupation of Kabul and other cities.

In 2001, the US government believed al-Qaeda, the radical Islamist group behind the September 11 attacks on the World Trade Centre in New York, had sanctuary in Afghanistan. The ultraconservative Taliban, in control of most of the country, refused to hand them over, and US forces invaded in December. The Taliban was overthrown, but re-emerged a few years later using improvised explosive devices (IEDs) and suicide bombs against the US-backed government in Kabul. When American forces withdrew from Afghanistan in August 2021, the national army trained by them was quickly overwhelmed. President Ashraf Ghani fled the country, and the Taliban regained control of most centres of population. As US military personnel and Afghan civilians were being evacuated from Kabul airport, they were attacked by militants affiliated with Islamic State (Daesh), which had wider international aims than the Taliban.

Peru, 1988

Throughout the 1980s, militants of Sendero Luminoso, the Shining Path Maoist revolutionary movement, were extremely active in Peru. The insurgents had strong support among the impoverished peasantry and indigenous people in the highlands. In February 1988, I travelled south from Ecuador down the Pacific Coast of Peru on buses. From Huarez, the bus up into the Cordillera de los Andes passed through picturesque villages. In a small mountain town, many local people and indigenous Indians lined the main street. Cold water splashed in my face as bags of it flew in through the windows. The whoops and shouts of onlookers could be heard above the pandemonium as soaked passengers laughed and screamed at the traditional welcome. As the bus headed higher up into the mountains, I succumbed to the increasing altitude and was repeatedly sick for an hour or so before we descended to Lima on the Pacific coast. When I walked across the Plaza Mayor in the centre of the city the next morning, there was a strong military presence with armoured vehicles and soldiers guarding the Palacio de Gobierno.

After a couple of days staying in an old colonial hotel near the main square and exploring old Lima, I booked a flight to Cuzco. Travelling there by bus was not possible because the regions of Ayacucho and Huancavelica were Sendero Luminoso strongholds. Peruvians also had to avoid those areas, and demand for flights was high. There were chaotic scenes at the airport with crowds of people in the departure hall and no discernible queueing system for check-in. As the scheduled departure time approached, it became clear that many people would not get on the flight. I got my ticket reallocated for a flight at the same time the next day, which fortunately took off on time with me on board. In Cuzco that evening, the atmosphere in the cobbled streets was buzzing with energy, heightened by rarefied air and the aptly named drink, pisco sour. A couple of days later, the small mountain train zig-zagged up from Cuzco on its way to Aguas Calientes, guarded by soldiers to deter attacks by Shining Path militants.

Remnants of the Sendero Luminoso guerrilla movement continued to clash with police and government soldiers in some highland areas until the 1990s. Alberto Fujimori, who was elected president of Peru in 1990, deregulated the economy and ruled with increasing authoritarianism. His 'war against terrorism' effectively ended the 'Shining Path' insurgency when its leader, Abimael Guzmán, was arrested in 1992 and sentenced to life in prison. He died on 11 September 2021 after refusing to eat. Fujimori served as president of Peru from 1990–2000, but was sentenced to 25 years in prison in 2009 for ordering massacres of alleged insurgents and for corruption. He died of cancer in 2024, coincidentally on 11 September, the anniversary of Guzmán's death.

During the COVID pandemic, the Peruvian government prioritised economic liberalism over prevention, much as President Trump did in the United States. Peru had one of the highest COVID death rates in the world at the time of the presidential election in June 2021. The campaign of the winning socialist candidate, Pedro Castillo, drew attention to the economic disparities between highland areas with a large indigenous population and the more prosperous coastal areas. Alberto Fujimori's daughter, Keiko, narrowly lost the second round to him and initiated a legal challenge to overturn the result.

High above Cuzco in 1988, the train climbed slowly beside the fast-flowing Urubamba River whose coffee-coloured waters tumbled down over rocks and boulders. From the end of the line at Aguas Calientes, it was a short hike the next morning up to the Inca ruins of Machu Picchu. Walking with two young Australian women I'd met on the train, we came under attack –not from militants but bees. The sting of a small killer bee can be no worse than that of a wasp, but they attack indiscriminately in swarms. One of my companions was physically sick when we finally got the bees out of her thick bushy hair. I sympathised after my experience on the bus over the Andes. Before going by bus up to Lake Titicaca at over 3,800 metres and to La Paz in Bolivia, I chewed coca leaves with lime like the locals to prevent mountain sickness.

Cameroon, 1986

The mini-buses that provided transport in much of Cameroon were known for eventful and light-hearted travel. Women chatted loudly as they bounced along bumpy mud tracks on their way home from the market. Most of the buses had signs on the walls inside informing passengers of strict rules. In addition to the ubiquitous no smoking sign 'Défense de fumer', there was another 'Défense de vomir'. Being sick on the bus was forbidden.

On the trip in 1986, I travelled by bus and minibus from the capital Yaoundé to a small village near Kribi on the Atlantic coast. After checking in at a small guest house, I went for a walk around the wooden huts and street stalls in the village. As usual in a small community, a white foreigner aroused curiosity, and I got talking to a tall Bantu lad called Daniel, who spoke good English. I'd read there were gorillas living in the rain forest along the River Campo near the border with Equatorial Guinea. Daniel said there were no buses or bush taxis going to Campo as there were no markets on the way. A few trucks did make the trip, and he agreed to ask around about a ride and go with me as a translator. I gave him a small amount of money to buy some food for the journey and arranged to meet him at the guest house at 6.30 the next morning.

I wasn't too surprised when Daniel didn't show up in the morning and went to ask at the tea stall where he lived. It was a small village and I soon found someone to show me to his hut. At the door, I called out, but there was no reply. I looked inside and saw him lying on a mattress, still wearing his clothes. I could smell the beer he'd spent my money on and shook him firmly. As his bleary eyes opened, I said, "Come on Daniel, we're going to look for gorillas. You're going to find me a truck." He was less keen in the light of a new day, but I got him to the tea stall for a drink. We heard that a small truck would be leaving soon for Campo, and found it nearby, stacked with crates of bottles full of fizzy drink. A few other passengers arrived, and we all climbed up to sit on the crates. The truck set off down a red-earth track through the forest to the sound of rattling bottles.

The Campo and Ma'an forests in the southwestern corner of Cameroon, bordering Equatorial Guinea to the south and the Atlantic

Ocean to the west, are home to a wide range of animals, including western lowland gorillas. The current Campo Ma'an National Park, created in 2000, is a World Bank Biodiversity Conservation and Management Project. The protected area was in part established to compensate for damage to biodiversity and the ecosystem caused by laying the Chad-Cameroon oil pipeline. It is important for the conservation of gorillas, which are now rare or absent altogether from areas with both logging and hunting. Many people living in the forest area work in the agro-industry or rubber and palm oil plantations. The indigenous Baka and Bagyeli forest people, widely referred to as 'pygmies', live by gathering, fishing and hunting using spears and traps. Unlike poachers involved in the illegal trade in wildlife who use guns, they have an in-depth knowledge and respect for the forest ecosystem and participate in its management.

After an hour or so swaying along precariously on top of the drinks truck, there was a loud *phshhhh* sound from below. All on board clambered down to inspect the flat tyre on the rear wheel. After some heated discussion in the local language, the driver's mate eventually hauled a spare wheel out of the cab. Relief was short-lived when the frayed outer edge of the tyre revealed a pink inner tube showing through. The wheel was quickly fitted, everyone clambered on board, and we set off again, lurching over bumps and holes in the dirt track. After no more than a few hundred metres, the jolting progress predictably ended with a loud bang! Only three wheels still had inflated tyres, and there was no spare wheel. We had passed no other vehicles along the track in either direction, and the prospects didn't look good. Even so, the driver seemed confident he could sort things out. The other passengers decided to leave him to get on with the job and walk along the track for a while.

Forest Walk

The atmosphere in the forest was enchanting with bird calls and monkeys chattering. Daniel assured me there were no dangerous animals in that part of the forest apart from snakes, and we followed the others walking in file and in silence. I was at the back and soon began to sense there was something behind me. When I looked back, I could see nothing along an empty track, so I thought my senses were playing tricks. A few metres further on, I turned my head again and this time saw a man walking close behind me who was little more than four feet high (1.20 metres), wearing just a loincloth and carrying a spear. It sent a shiver down my spine, but I just nodded my head to acknowledge his presence. Looking ahead again, I saw Daniel had been joined by three or four other 'pygmies' who had emerged silently from the forest. After a while, they veered off to the left along a narrow track, indicating that the two of us should follow. I had read about the Baka people who live in the forest, but had not expected to see them and had no idea what this diversion would lead to.

A short distance further on, we emerged into a clearing with some grass huts. A few 'pygmies', both men and women, were standing outside. An old man, who barely came up to my elbow, walked towards me and took me gently by the arm. He led me to a large rectangular hut made of sticks and grass, which I took to be the communal meeting place. On entering, I saw a wooden platform like a trestle table in the middle of the room. As the old man guided me towards it, I saw an old woman lying there. I looked at her wrinkled face and her closed eyes – she was dead. I turned to the old man who may have been her husband and shook my head slowly. "I'm very sorry," I said, the words inadequate, and

I'm not sure he understood. I wondered if the 'pygmies' had mistaken me for a white man who had visited the village before, perhaps an anthropologist or health worker. The old man looked very sad but dignified. I put my hand on his shoulder and said we had to leave. I walked back to the path leading to the road, feeling a bit stunned and sorry for the man and the whole village.

Back on the dirt road, we reached the other passengers and heard sounds from another world –an engine running and bottles rattling. The drinks truck appeared around the bend. Cheerful passengers ran to clamber onto the crates, and we set off again through the forest, African style.

'Porcupig'

Later in the afternoon, we reached the settlement near the Rio Campo, where we got a meal and beds for the night. We even had a litre bottle of beer each to go with the stew. I was told the meat was 'porcupig', and later confirmed it was an old word for porcupine. My 'guide' said we should get up at 4 o'clock the next morning and walk to a track through the forest where two Japanese zoologists usually drove by on their way to study the gorillas. By 8 o'clock, there was no sign of zoologists or gorillas, but a truck came along that could take us back up the coast to Kribi. In the evening, I walked from my guest house towards the smell of wood smoke coming from roadside stalls. I sat on a low stool while a young woman wearing a brightly coloured head wrap cooked a delicious meal on a charcoal fire, fresh fish with corn on the cob, and a large bottle of beer cooled in a bucket of rapidly melting ice.

Marriage Proposal

Travelling in Cameroon, I ate mostly grilled chicken, fish, or goat stew with corn on the cob. Maize and millet grew in the villages of the central region, where rainfall and sunshine are reliable. Clusters of thatched grass huts were almost hidden among the tall crops when I went to look around a typical village there. I'd walked several kilometres one morning while the sun got hotter, and received a friendly greeting from a young man in jeans and a T-shirt who spoke fluent French and some English. A teacher in the nearby town where I'd stayed the night before, he was visiting relatives still living a traditional rural life in the village, growing maize and millet and rearing a few goats and chickens. I was welcome to stay the night in a grass hut that was empty, and someone would cook me a meal if I paid for the whole chicken.

I sat outside the hut enjoying a drink of maize beer and chatting about the difference between life in a village and in the town. A young boy chased a chicken around a nearby hut, and I guessed it might be some time before I ate. It was late in the afternoon, but still quite hot, so I retreated to the cooler interior of the hut to rest before dinner. It wasn't long before I heard a woman's voice nearby, ululating loudly, a high-pitched yodel like the war cry of a Native American Indian in an old Hollywood movie. Outside, I saw a woman standing a few metres away, maybe thirty years old, completely naked and looking towards me. My French-speaking host arrived, and I asked what the noise was all about. It was a proposal. I'd heard the ululating sound before when walking on my own around the Dali-esque rock formations and orange sand dunes of the Wadi Rum desert in Jordan. Bedouin tribes live there with their camels, but they were nowhere to be seen, and that young woman kept herself well-hidden.

Travelling and later working in Africa, I was often asked questions about marriage and family in my country. The topic usually followed the question, "Where do you come from?" when a friendly conversation started. When I was with a female companion, the question was, "How many children do you have?", to which I would reply honestly that we didn't have any. The usual response to that was a sympathetic, "Oh, I'm sorry," as if I'd told them a close relative had died. When travelling on my own, African men would ask, "Where are your wives?"

Abubumbi II, the Fon of Bafut, has forty wives and rules over a small kingdom of about 120,000 people in the town of Bafut and its surrounding area. One of his many children will become his successor, but not necessarily the oldest child, as in European hereditary monarchies. The Fon will choose the most competent for the role after consultation with the elders. His father chose him despite being child number 302. He told an interviewer in 2015 that the Fon's main role these days was keeping the peace and promoting local development. He recognised the challenge of preserving traditional culture while being open to modern ideas and Western ways that are attractive to the young. His educational priorities were vocational training and development of craft skills that could give young people opportunities to earn a living.[9]

I'd taken a minibus to Bafut from Bamenda before going to Lake Nyos. After finding a guest house, I walked along narrow red-earthed lanes past small thatched houses with peach-coloured walls made of mud and straw. In an open area at the side of the palace grounds, there was a row of cottages with tiled roofs and walls of pink plaster where some of the Fon's wives lived. Behind was another row of cottages and the tall thatched pyramid roof of the central wooden shrine. The setting was peaceful in the welcome shade of leafy trees, and the pastel colours and architecture blended with houses in the area.

Back in the centre of the village, I met Chris, a young American Peace Corps volunteer, and we sat outside a tea shop for a drink and a chat. He said people in the area were superstitious and believed in witchcraft, but he was hopeful his project to build a secular primary school would be approved. He had arranged for the Fon to come to his house that afternoon to discuss the project, and as the Fon had attended school in England, I was welcome to join them. At his house, Chris set out cups and saucers and plates of biscuits on a coffee table. The Fon arrived punctually with one of his young wives and gave the impression of being modern, open-minded and progressive. He strongly supported the plan to build a new school, spoke knowledgeably about international affairs, and didn't ask about my wives.

Indonesia, 2010

Marriage between distant cousins ensures strong kinship bonds and support networks among the Toraja people in the central highlands of South Sulawesi on the island of Celebes (Sulawesi), one of the largest Indonesian islands. Cultural traditions have survived in Tana Toraja despite many of its people converting to Christianity.

I first heard about Tana Toraja from Lorna, a friend in Bangladesh who'd lived in China before she came to work in Dhaka. When I'd returned to England from Dhaka and was no longer working full-time, I flew to the verdant volcanic island of Bali in the Indonesian Archipelago in

2010. The aim was to visit some of the islands I'd missed when I sailed directly from Timor to Bali on my overland journey back to England from Australia in 1969–70. This time, travelling east on boats and buses, I spent a few days each on the islands of Bali, Lombok, Sumbawa and Flores. While on Flores, I learned that a boat would be leaving in a few days' time for Makassar, the main port in the south of Celebes. After a humid overnight crossing from Maumere and a more restful night in a guest house in Makassar, I took the long bus ride up into the spectacular highlands of South Sulawesi. In Rantapao, the main town in Tana Toraja, I rented a small wooden bungalow surrounded by tropical vegetation and spent a few days exploring some of the nearby area on foot.

The villages of the Toraja are each home to an extended family sharing ancestral houses called tongkonan. Relatives provide support for house building, farming and ceremonies. Christian converts do not perform some of the rituals, but funerals are conducted in accordance with an animistic belief system, aluk to dolo – the way of the ancestors. The traditional belief of Torajans is that the deceased requires a buffalo for the journey to puya, the afterlife, and elaborate funeral ceremonies involve animal sacrifice, feasting, music and dancing. [10]

A few miles south of Rantapao, I hiked through lush green fields where water buffalo wallowed in deep ponds. The roofs of robust wooden houses curved up at each end like the prow of a Spanish galleon. In the village of Londa, coffins had been suspended by ropes down the face of a high cliff to prevent theft of personal items inside. Other coffins were mostly in rock locations – natural caves, tombs hollowed out of giant boulders blasted from volcanoes long ago, and alcoves cut by hand into the cliff face. Half-sized wooden effigies (tau tau) of deceased ancestors sat or stood in balconies carved into the rock, 'theatre boxes' above the world's stage. Outstretched arms and upturned hands seemed to welcome the living or offer them refuge. Many figures clearly represented the poor dressed in rags, tattered trousers ripped at the knees and old cotton shirts shredded to dirty ribbons. Tight-lipped faces lacked distinctive character, although one man had a gag over his mouth. Wealthier people could afford skilled craftsmen, and their effigies were more life-like with recognizably individual faces and paler skin. Some were seated in separate 'theatre boxes' and appeared dressed in style for a special occasion.

The Way of the Ancestors

At the entrance to a large cave, I was greeted warmly by a local Torajan man who offered to show me around with a small lamp. When my eyes adjusted to the gloom, I saw coffins in shadowy corners and skulls resting on rock ledges in the nooks and crannies. A skeletal arm hung down the outside of a simple wooden coffin in a recess cut into the rock. Broken bits of old coffins, skulls and bones littered the ground, most likely shaken from their resting place by earth tremors. I asked my guide how he felt about walking among the bones of dead ancestors, past coffins of those he may have known personally. "I'm among friends," he said, and asked if I'd like to see another cave. He showed me a tunnel that led to it and to a different way out, which seemed more interesting than going back the same way. The opening was about a metre wide and half a metre high, but the tunnel soon narrowed to a less comfortable size. It had been cut by Torajans, who are smaller than most Europeans, and my shoulders are broad.

Progress through the tunnel was only possible lying face down, using elbows and toes to push along. Passage through the underworld was slow and claustrophobic. I realised there was no going back and had no idea how far it was to the next cave. To distract my mind from thoughts of getting stuck or the tunnel collapsing, I tried to focus on the restricted movements that kept me slowly inching forward. My guide's lamp, a few metres in front, lit the way ahead in otherwise total darkness. Eventually, it shone on the wall of a cave, and I squeezed out, relieved to stand again. Skeletons and separated skulls with empty eye sockets lay around – some ghoulish grey, others yellow or brown with age. In a recess, three skulls in a row rested chinless and toothless on a ledge. Walking through broken coffins and scattered bones, we reached the mouth of the cave and emerged into dazzling sunlight and the land of the living.

France, 2008

Deep inside the vast cave complex *Grotte de Niaux* in the French Pyrenees, spooky shadows flitted along the walls, cast by the lamps of people walking along a subterranean river bed. On the walls of a huge rock chamber, animals had been drawn with immense skill and attention to scale. A vertical line on the side of a bison looked like a spear hanging down. Arrows on the side of other animals could have been added to the original artwork, and it wasn't clear what they indicated.

Costa Rica, 2009

At a fork in a track through the Monteverde rainforest in Costa Rica, an arrow on a wooden signpost pointed to the right. The words, 'Solo Caminata Nocturna,' suggested the trail was for hiking at night with a torch to see nocturnal animals. In the afternoon, there was little daylight and no visible animal life. I'd walked for an hour or so through dense forest, hearing but not seeing birds in the thick canopy. Suddenly, a shaft of sunlight pierced through the trees, lighting up the sign a few metres ahead. I stopped in my tracks as a flurry of feathers was caught in the spotlight. A spectacular green and turquoise bird, a motmot, landed on the sign, its iridescent head and wings shining in the sun. We watched each other in silence for a while till it flew off through the trees. I branched left along a path that soon led out of the dark forest. In the open again, I felt heavy spots of warm rain, but the lush green valley below was bathed in sunlight. A rainbow arched over the village of Santa Elena and its cluster of buildings with roofs painted red, green or blue.

England, 2009

Costa Rica emerged from the sea millions of years ago when the Earth's crust crumpled under tectonic pressure. Some volcanoes remain active, and earthquakes are common. In Britain, only minor earthquakes occur, although the mountainous landscape in the north was formed by volcanic eruptions and shaped over millions of years by the elements. In recent times, weather systems have brought warm, moist air from the Atlantic to the mountains of Cumbria in the north-west of England, making it the wettest place in the country.

Rain clouds loomed heavy over the green hills of Cumbria as I drove along a narrow, windswept road flanked by a drystone wall. A gap ahead looked wide enough to drive through onto flat ground where I could park – it had been a long journey. The hill beside the road promised a rewarding view despite the threat of rain. Climbing quickly along a track made by sheep or hikers, I soon looked down on a toy-sized car. Rain did begin to fall, light at first, then stinging with hail on the windy side of the hill. At the top, the rain stopped. Bright sunlight broke through gaps in the dense dark clouds. An ephemeral arc of pure colour spanned the rusty orange remnants of last year's bracken, the lush green lowlands, and a blue-grey lake far below. The way down looked steeper than the way I'd come up, but I could get back to where I started from before it rained anymore.

In a small village in Cumbria, a river flows down from the hills. White water rushes beneath a grey stone bridge, spreading out into a swirling pool. Just downstream by a grassy bank, wild trout rest in the calm, clear water of the shallows. Reflections of clouds ripple on the surface as the river flows by.

Epilogue

Heavy and prolonged rain fell in Cumbria in November 2009, with 316 mm (12.4 inches) recorded in twenty-four hours. Cockermouth town centre was under two metres of water. [11] *For the UK as a whole, records of average daily rainfall dating back to 1862 indicate that the wettest February, April, June, November and December months were after 2009.* [12] *When Storm Desmond struck in December 2015, the River Derwent burst its banks, causing extensive damage to homes and businesses in Cockermouth despite an additional barrier built after the floods in 2009. A record 341 mm of rain (13 inches) fell in twenty-four hours in Cumbria.* [13]

These floods in Cumbria were the biggest in over 550 years, according to research on lake sediments. [14] *Extreme floods had not been common in the past, and the recent cluster was associated with higher temperatures. The ten warmest years in the UK since records of average daily temperature began in 1884 were in the first two decades of the 21st century. The decade 2010–19 was 1°C warmer on average than the period 1961–90.* [12] *Evidence suggests that higher temperatures are affecting rainfall patterns around the world. Some regions are becoming drier with adverse consequences for water supplies, agriculture and wildfires, while other areas are becoming wetter.* [15]

England, 2020

Heavy rain fell in Cumbria again when Storm Ciara arrived in 2020. Warm air from the mid-Atlantic flowed inland on the prevailing westerly wind, rising up when it reached the mountains. As the air cooled, it condensed, and the rain fell on already saturated ground. In one twenty-four-hour period in February 2020, 177 mm (7 inches) of rain were recorded in Cumbria. [16] *It was the wettest February in England and Wales since records began in 1766.*[12]

Devastating as the floods in 2020 were for people in Cumbria and many parts of England and Wales, the year will be remembered for events that affected everyone. By the Easter holiday period, when the Cumbria National Park would normally be visited by thousands of people, it was closed, not because of flooding but to prevent transmission of a dangerous new virus.

The COVID-19 pandemic demonstrated the disastrous global consequences when a new severe infectious disease emerges and transmits rapidly between large populations with air transport links. In this case, a coronavirus was identified as the causal agent, later named SARS-CoV-2, but hundreds of new pathogens have been identified in human populations since the 1940s. Many have transferred from other species (zoonotic), causing new infectious diseases. [17] *Recent ecological research has shown that new threats emerge when humans disturb or clear natural habitats.*

Disruption of wildlife habitats is often the result of unrestrained or illegal economic activity, and large areas of pristine forest in Africa, Asia and South America have been destroyed. Clearing the forest reduces the population of large animals, makes new areas accessible for hunting smaller animals that can carry pathogens harmful to humans, such as monkeys,[18] *and may increase numbers of rodents, bats and birds from which harmful pathogens can transfer to humans.*[19] *In some parts of the world, the incidence of insect-borne, water-borne, and food-borne infectious diseases has also increased due to recent climatic changes.*[20]

Significant progress has been made in protecting people from infectious diseases, and the threat from emerging diseases is under constant surveillance.[21] However, many economic activities continue to damage health and natural habitats. Large-scale agriculture, logging, mining, road building, many industries and wars cause environmental damage, while pesticides, plastics, oil, chemicals and sewage pollute the seas, rivers and soil, causing disease through contamination of drinking water and food. Livestock, rotting organic material, extracting shale gas, and burning natural gas produce methane, which contributes to global heating. Burning fossil fuels and biofuels produces other greenhouse gases including carbon dioxide, disrupting the climate and polluting the air with particulates which cause chronic respiratory disease. [22] Improvements have been made despite opposition from powerful groups protecting their economic interest.[23] Without effective control of large-scale economic activities there will be further damage to the planet, the climate, and people's health. Cooperative action at the local, national and international levels can prevent further degradation of the natural environment, while measures to restore ecosystems and support biodiversity foster a healthier relationship with nature and the planet as a whole.

Notes

1. Nigel Barley. The Innocent Anthropologist. Harmondsworth: Penguin Books, 1983.
2. Erich Kästner. Emile and the Detectives. London: Vintage, 2012.
3. George Arney. Afghanistan. London: Mandarin, 1990, pp 249–256.
4. Jamie McGuinness. Trekking in the Everest Region. Hindhead, Surrey, UK: Trailblazer Publications, 2000, p 24.
5. Centres for Disease Control and Prevention, National Vital Statistics Reports, 2019; 68 (9).
6. Seaman J, Mercer AJ, Sondorp E. 'The epidemic of visceral leishmaniasis in Western Upper Nile, Southern Sudan: course and impact 1984 to 1994'. International Journal of Epidemiology, 1996; 25 (4): 862–871.
7. Editors of the Encyclopaedia Britannica. 'Indian Ocean Tsunami of 2004'. Article online updated 29 September, 2025.
8. The Rubáiyát of Omar Kayyám. Rendered into English Verse by Edward J Fitzgerald. New York: Airmont, 1970.
9. 'Fon Abumbi II – Bafut Kingdom'. Interview on YouTube, 2016.
10. Terence W Bigalke. Tana Toraja: A Social History of Indonesian People. Singapore: Singapore University Press, 2005.
11. UK Met Office. 'Heavy rainfall/flooding in the Lake District, Cumbria – November 2009'.

12. Mike Kendon, et al. 'State of the UK Climate 2020'. International Journal of Climatology, 2021; 41 (S2): 3–4.
13. UK Met Office. 'Flooding in Cumbria December 2015'; 'Storm Desmond'.
14. Chiverrel RC, et al. 'Using lake sediment archives to improve understanding of flood magnitude and frequency: recent extreme flooding in northwest UK'. Earth Surface Processes and Landforms, 2019; 44: 2366–2376.
15. UK Met Office. 'UK and global extreme events – drought'.
16. UK Met Office. 'Storm Ciara'.
17. Jones KE, et al. 'Global trends in emerging infectious diseases', Nature, 2008; 451: 990–994. doi:10.1038/nature06536.
18. Peeters M, et al. 'Risk to human health from a plethora of simian immunodeficiency viruses in primate bushmeat'. Emerging Infectious Diseases, 2002; 8: 451–457.
19. Obstfeld RS and Keesing F. 'Species that can make us ill thrive in human habitats.' Nature, 2020; 584: 346–347.
20. Anikeeva O, et al. 'The impact of increasing temperatures due to climate change on infectious diseases'. British Medical Journal, 2024; 387: e079343.
21. Alexander Mercer. 'Protection against severe infectious disease in the past.' Pathogens and Global Health, 2021 May; 115 (3): 151–167. doi.org/10.1080/20477724.2021.1878443.

22. Fuller R, et al. 'Pollution and health: a progress update. Lancet Planet Health. 2022; 6: e535-e547. doi: 10.1016/S2542-5196(22)00090-0.
23. David Michaels, The Triumph of Doubt. Dark Money and the Science of Deception. Oxford and New York: Oxford University Press, 2020, pp 266–272.

Everest Range from Geu La, Tibet, 2000

Everest Trail, Pangboche, Nepal, 2002

Everest in Clouds near Rongphu, Tibet, 2000

Everest from Kala Patar, Nepal, 2002

Torres Del Paine, Chile, 2008

Perito Merino Glacier, Argentina, 2008

Torres Del Paine, Chile, 2008

Perito Merino Glacier, Argentina, 2008

Kabul, Afghanistan, 1970

Kathmandu, Nepal, 1970

Herat, Afghanistan, 1970

Sydney, Australia, 2001

Rashaida, Showak, Sudan, 1990

Afghan Buzkashi, Peshawar, Pakistan, 1992

The Nile near Luxor, 1983

Jaisalmer, Rajasthan, India, 2012

About the Author

Alec Mercer was born in Leicester, where he lived until he left school and went to university in London. Despite the cultural and political turbulence of the 1960s and early 1970s, and the lure of travel, he eventually focused more productively on important health and population issues. Through further studies in demography and research on health data, he developed skills he later applied in some of the low-income countries visited in his youth. After several years working in Africa and Asia, he returned to England to resume independent research on changing disease patterns, before embarking on this very different literary project.

Printed in Dunstable, United Kingdom